THE ART OF
RISK

Also by this author

This Is Your Brain on Sex

THE ART OF
RISK

The New Science
of Courage,
Caution, & Chance

KAYT SUKEL

NATIONAL GEOGRAPHIC

Washington, D.C.

Published by the National Geographic Society
1145 17th Street NW, Washington, DC 20036

Library of Congress Cataloging-in-Publication Data

Sukel, Kayt.
  The art of risk : the new science of courage, caution, and chance / Kayt Sukel.
    pages cm
Includes bibliographical references and index.
ISBN 978-1-4262-1472-1 (hardcover : alk. paper)
1. Risk-taking (Psychology) I. Title.
BF637.R57S85 2016
155.9--dc23

                        2015010776

Interior design: Melissa Farris
Printed in the United States of America
15/QGF-CML/1

For Ella.

I'm betting on you, kiddo.

CONTENTS

PART I

RISK, NOW AND THEN

Chapter One

....

CONFESSIONS OF A REFORMED RISK-TAKER

ONCE UPON A TIME, I WAS A RISK-TAKER. For most of my life, in fact, I was known as such. Even when I was a toddler, I'm told, the word most often used to describe me, by family and strangers alike, was "fearless." There was no tree too high to climb, no puzzle too hard to solve, and no peer too intimidating to approach. That quality stayed with me as I grew into adulthood. As a teen and a young adult, I usually responded to any dare with "Why not?" I climbed mountains, swam with sharks (both literally and figuratively), hiked desolate trails, traveled extensively, and jumped out of perfectly good airplanes. I fell in love more times than I could count, eventually marrying a soldier during a time of war, and then moved across the Atlantic to live with him—and have a baby—in

Europe. While he was deployed to Iraq, I could have come back to the States to find a job or stay with family. You know, the predictable response to being left on your own for a year with an infant. Instead, I strapped my young child on my back and headed out to explore Europe, the Middle East, and Africa. Later, I divorced that soldier, moved back to the States, and started over from scratch. I immersed myself in researching and writing a book about love and sex—and even had an orgasm in a functional magnetic resonance imaging scanner (and then watched that orgasm go viral on the Internet). And that's just the highlight reel. Time and time again, I faced challenges head-on (and often dealt with less-than-ideal immediate outcomes) to fully immerse myself in the world.

For the better part of my life, you see, I threw my arms open to possibility and embraced risk—thinking my "fearless" nature played a big part in my successes. I tallied my big mistakes, both professional and personal, like notches on a headboard, believing that my foibles offered me as much, if not more, than my achievements when it came to reaching my potential.

But now? I'm no longer so certain. I'm not sure I'd classify the place I'm currently at—a bored, single mom living in the suffocating confines of suburbia—as success, exactly. And frankly, when I look closely at my situation, it doesn't seem all that different from where my more play-it-safe type of friends ended up. But one thing is clear: Somewhere along the line, while taking all those risks and tallying up all those mistakes, I lost my mojo. These days, I'm no longer looking for my next adventure. The only thing I seem to be looking for is the next *Law and Order* marathon on cable. I appear to be suffering from a "reverse midlife crisis." Instead of approaching my 40s with a 22-year-old boy toy and a Corvette, I've joined the PTA and bought myself a nice, reliable station wagon. When I take a hard look, I realize I'm now much more of a spectator than a participant in life. And it bothers me. A lot. But not enough, thus far, to do anything about it.

I am not sure what has changed in the past few years to cause this reverse midlife crisis. Could it be my environment? My age? My gender? Exhaustion? The responsibilities involved in single motherhood—or perhaps just motherhood in general? A raw and battered psyche after a painstaking divorce? A lack of crazy peers whispering the right kind of suggestions in my ear? A newfound fear of consequences? Or is some other factor at play? I can't be sure of the answer.

But I need to find out. Because I find myself at a bit of a cross-roads—in both my professional and personal lives. And if risk-taking was a key component of my success in the past, I need to find a way to harness it in my future.

You see, my work life is not where I want it to be. Like many of my peers, I seem to err on the side of playing it safe when it comes to my career. With retirement lurking on the horizon, fixing me with terrifying, not-good-enough, you're-going-to-die-broke-and-alone type stares, it's hard to imagine a career path these days where you can forgo safety. Especially when you have a child counting on you—paying the bills (and paying the bills in a place with a decent public school system) seems nonnegotiable. But safety, especially as a writer, is *tedious*. Yet tedium often seems to be the required trade-off for getting the mortgage paid each month.

Perhaps I wouldn't feel so bad about work if I didn't feel like safety was also unduly influencing other aspects of my life, especially when it comes to love. Since my divorce, I've avoided romantic entanglements like the plague. I've dated plenty—and managed to sustain a few pseudo-relationships with artfully constructed boundaries here and there. But those boundaries extinguished the possibility of a real connection. While many of the men I met were amazing people, I made sure to always keep them at a distance—literally. I found myself gravitating toward men who lived far, far outside my zip code. This made it easy for me to never introduce them to my son or my family. This made it possible for me to never invite any of them to my city let alone my home. This offered me the potential to do it all on my own terms. And this all but guaranteed I'd never have to worry about approaching any kind of intimacy. My strict rules kept me safe and those men separate. And as soon as anyone hinted at the possibility of a commitment, or tried to push the careful limits I had set, I did my best, one way or another, to make sure the entire liaison fell apart.

But then I met someone who has me rethinking my approach. In fact, in less than a month, I've broken all my rules for him. And I've done so without a second thought. Not to sound like some kind of vapid schoolgirl, but he makes my heart go pitter-patter in the most teenage of ways. Since we've met, he's somehow managed to impress my mother, charm my son, and get repeated invites to my home. And just last week he told me, "I intend to marry you, if you'll have me. The sooner the better." And while I did not immediately reply to such a spook-worthy statement, I did not think he was completely crazy for saying it out loud either. Even, despite realizing, when I counted back in my head, that we had known each other for only six weeks.

So, you can see why a better understanding of risk is feeling quite personal right now. Sure, safety is, well, *safe,* but will it help me achieve the things I really want for my life? Do I change up my work business model and start doing more projects that I'm passionate about, even if it may adversely affect my bottom line (and, in turn, my ability to pay for home maintenance and soccer cleats)? Do I consider the possibility of marrying again, especially so soon, even though my first trip down the aisle ended in such disaster? And how can I even begin to calculate how marriage, whether it fails or succeeds, may affect my child? Should getting out of my comfort zone become more of a priority? I have a lot of responsibilities—and a lot at stake. So how can I make the most of the risk in my choices so that I reap the benefits, as opposed to suffer the consequences?

Once upon a time, I was a risk-taker. And as I consider what I want for my future, I think I'd like to be one again. But this time around, I'd like to learn how to be a *smart* risk-taker. After all, I have more to protect than just myself now: a child, a house, my professional and personal reputation, my savings, and my heart. I know a sports car and a meaningless fling won't make me happy. But I have an inkling that more invigorating work, a good relationship, and a happy child might. And as I face the current risks in my own life, I see that there are myriad variables that influence them. But it's unclear which of those I should be paying attention to in order to make optimal choices.

Psychologists have been studying the art of decision-making for centuries. And I use the word "art" intentionally. Because the pervasive takeaway from much of this work is that human beings are pretty bad at making good (or, at least, rational) decisions when faced with risk. We are terrible at calculating the actual probabilities of specific outcomes. We hate ambiguity to the point where we just pretend it doesn't exist. We would rather hear a good story than bother with a not-so-good reality. We can tell you the difference between cause and correlation but aren't so interested in practically applying it. Simply put, when it comes time to make a decision, especially one involving risk, we have a tendency to focus on the wrong factors. We are susceptible to a variety of decision-making biases and heuristics, or shortcuts, that too often lead us astray.

But I don't want to be led astray! I want to be able to properly vet risk. I want to have a good understanding of when it makes sense to push forward and when it's better to play it safe. I want to recognize what factors influenced my past risk-taking behaviors (the good and the bad)—and to ascertain what ones may be holding me back now. And I'd like some direction, if it's not too much to ask. I'd like to know what I need to be paying attention to in life's more pressing situations—those proverbial crossroads, if you will— that determine our personal and professional successes.

It's likely you'd appreciate knowing these things too. And scientists are hoping to find the answers to some of those very questions using a new field of inquiry.

Today, the more specific field of *decision neuroscience,* an assembly of psychological, management, economic, genetic, epidemiological, evolutionary science, and neurobiological studies, is attempting to shed light on what is happening in our brains as we make decisions—and how, where, and why we stray from the optimal as we decide. Researchers are learning about all the ways different genes, neurochemicals, brain circuits, phenotypes, and hormones influence how we approach risky business.

Particular focus is on the mesocortical limbic pathway, a sophisticated circuit that links the basal ganglia, a cluster of subcortical regions near the brain stem, to the brain's emotional and memory centers as well as the prefrontal cortex, the area of the brain responsible for executive control. This unique configuration of brain regions is often described as a "reward" processing circuit. But that's not exactly right. Craig Ferris, a noted neuroscientist at Northeastern University, describes it as the brain's motivation system. "It evaluates the risks and rewards involved with certain behaviors," he says. "It's also involved with calculating the predictability of things that may come if you engage in a particular behavior."

Risks *and* rewards. So here is a brain circuit that may offer us great insights on how the brain weighs risks and how those calculations end up influencing our behavior. But while neuroscientists are often the first to tell you that the brain *is* behavior—that the brain directs literally every step we take, every decision we make—understanding a particular brain pathway seldom offers concrete advice on how to do something better. And even when it seems there might be some good intelligence wrapped in a particular finding, it's not always easy to know just where and how you should apply it.

Because while many of us fear risk (at least I seem to these days), we applaud risk-takers. We pay homage to heroes, rule-breakers, and thrill-seekers each and every day. These are the men and women who inspire us with tales of derring-do—they make our lives better by challenging the status quo, rushing into burning buildings, shaping new boundaries, creating new technologies, climbing the most dangerous peaks, and doing the (seemingly) impossible. They are favored protagonists in novels and movies— and, in real life, the faces prominently featured on our favorite magazines. These are the people who make us believe that any-thing—anything!—is possible. And even the most risk-averse among us aspire to their success.

So, science may provide us with some much needed answers. But let's face it: While science, especially brain science, makes a lot of implicit promises, those promises aren't always delivered when it counts. Generally, you won't find specific instruction on how to improve, well, anything, hidden within the jargon of a scientific treatise. As someone who is hoping to learn how to approach risk better in the future, to find some of that success that heralded risk-takers have found by taking a few big gambles, I want more than just some facts and findings. I want to know how those results should be applied in the real world. I want to know what factors I need to pay attention to in order to make a good decision. I want to know how I should be viewing both opportu-nities and mistakes to maximize my success in the future. Simply put, I want to know how successful risk-takers are doing it—what particular blend of biology and experience held within allows them to know what risks are worth taking and what risks should be left alone. You might be curious about that too.

In the following chapters, I will explore the new and fascinating research on risk-taking and how it influences human decision-making—in work, in play, in love, and in life. You'll learn more about the parts of the brain that have been implicated in risk-taking; the different genes and neurochemicals, those neurotransmitters and other molecules involved with brain function, that influence how we weigh different factors as we take those risks; and the complex interplay of biological and environmental variables that may help some of us better navigate risky situations.

I'll also talk to real-world risk-takers, those who have gambled it all and still gone on to achieve great victory, to put those findings in context. I'll ask individuals who deal with risk on a regular basis—people like professional poker player Andy Frankenberger, military family advocate Kristina Kaufmann, neurosurgeon David Baskin, and professional free solo climber and BASE jumper Steph Davis—how their brains translate uncertainty into potential in the real world. And I'll look at how the ways they perceive and manage factors like preparation, stress, emotion, failure, and social pressure can help the rest of us as we encounter risk in our own lives.

Every day, each of us will make thousands of decisions—many of which we may not even be conscious of. And every one of those decisions, monumental or trivial, carries with it some element of risk. I want to understand where the science meets success when it comes to evaluating and acting on those risks. Because there are lessons to be learned at the intersection of the laboratory and the real world: Lessons that can show us where, when, and how it makes sense to take a risk. Lessons to guide our attention and focus as we consider all the factors—and there are plenty of 'em—influencing a particularly risky decision. And, with luck, lessons regarding how we might best take advantage of the risky opportunities in our own lives, even if we find ourselves to now be somewhat risk-averse, to realize our most cherished dreams.

Once upon a time, I was a risk-taker. And as I consider my next moves in life, I hope I might become a risk-taker again. But as I move forward, I intend to be a more informed one.

Chapter Two

WHAT IS RISK ANYWAY?

FROM A DISTANCE, GAYLE KING, a 65-year-old asphalt scientist hailing from Galveston, Texas, might look like the kind of man who avoids risk at all costs.

In fact, he'll be the first one to tell you that he's simply not all that open to change. Rather, King is the kind of person who appreciates staying the course. He has been happily married to the same woman for more than 40 years. (And he's worn the same familiar, bushy mustache for equally as long.) His usual daily uniform consists of comfortable shoes and Hawaiian-style shirts in muted prints—a wardrobe of shirts so similar that, at holiday dinners, his family has actually debated where and when he picked up a particular specimen. He has traveled the world but prefers to do so from the comfortable sanctuary of a cruise ship. A Midwesterner at heart, he believes in hard work and good manners. And, more important, he actively practices both. He is good-natured and even-keeled in the most stressful of circumstances. Now in his mid-60s, King could fully retire from a long and successful career and live the easy life. But he prefers to keep working, albeit now on more of a part-time basis—appreciating the stability of a regular paycheck. As I said, from a distance, Gayle King might look like the kind of man who avoids risk at all costs. But he knows more than a thing or two about it. He grew up on a sprawling family farm in rural Ohio. Watching his parents run such a high-risk venture, he knew early on in life that farming wasn't for him.

"There's no certainty at all in it. It's really high risk and high stress," he says, citing weather, government, and the farming commodities market as just a few of the unknowns that can affect a farmer's bottom line. It's also fairly dangerous work. While farming might not seem like the most exciting of vocations, both animal and grain farmers are regulars on "Deadliest Profession" lists, with a significant number of job-related injuries and deaths each year.

Given the high risks involved with farm life, King instead wanted a job that would afford him stability and security. And he did his homework. When it came time to head off to college, he settled on one of the safest career paths he knew: chemistry.

"When I went into the field, you could count on a job. You could project what your salary would be within a certain range, depending on your education and experience," he says, leaning back in his chair on a sprawling patio overlooking the beach and tapping his fingers on his stomach. "You could even look up those numbers in the back of *Chemistry* magazine. And once I got my degree, I got a job that fit right into what I expected. It was about as close to a sure thing as you could get back then, provided you put in the work and effort."

King has taken that kind of approach to most of the decisions in his life. He's looked up the numbers, crunched them as much as he is able, and then made a decision based on the result. "So much of any risk is really just looking at the statistics," he says confidently. And he attributes much of his success in life to his ability to run those statistics and make sound, secure decisions based on the results.

The way King explains risk is nearly identical to the way economists have described it ever since they started studying it empirically. Back in the day, risk wasn't about trekking to the top of Mount Everest, drinking to blackout, or racing down a dark and winding road at 100 miles per hour. Rather, it was a simple concept used to quantify the probability of a particular outcome in a decision-making task.

King is a rational man, a logical man. He puts his faith in mathematics. He even describes himself as "overanalytical, at times"—though he finds great comfort in approaching decisions in an analytical fashion. Not many of us make decisions the way that King does. I know I don't. (But, King himself doesn't always adhere to a strict numbers game when it comes to decision-making either—more on that later).

A CHANGING DEFINITION

....

Consider a simple decision-making task. Such a task might involve something like a coin flip. If the coin lands heads up, you win a dollar. If it's tails, you walk away with nothing. In this case, the risk, economically speaking, is clear. You have a 50-50 chance of adding a dollar to your wallet. Easy, right? The risk, or probability that you will win a dollar, is 50 percent. There's no potential for real loss—unless you decide to count a dollar you never actually had. Rather, here you have a situation in which you know the probability of all your possible outcomes. And with 50-50 odds, why not play?

But what might happen if you change up that scenario a bit? Say you are offered 50 cents just for saying hello. Or you can have the opportunity to double that money with the coin flip. Once again, heads gets you a dollar. Tails, a total loss. Now risk becomes a bit more complicated. You have a choice between walking away 50 cents richer for doing nothing but saying, "No, thank you," or taking a gamble for the possibility of a dollar. Now you have to decide between a guaranteed (but lesser) payout or a double-or-nothing gamble. Which would you chose?

Despite a guaranteed windfall, most people will try for the dollar. After all, the stakes aren't that high, and the probability of winning remains at 50 percent. But what happens when you change the game? Up the stakes? Delay the payout? Play multiple times? Compete against your friends—or your boss, or your significant other, or that super-hottie who works with your sister? What might happen if you add an emotional component to the game?

Or a little extra stress? Or if you flip after making a few errors on a seemingly unrelated task? That's exactly what economists, psychologists, and neuroscientists have been looking at over the past few decades. They've taken a simple numbers game, changed up the many variables, and watched how people's decision-making behaviors have changed in response.

Joshua Buckholtz, a neuroscientist at Harvard University who studies decision-making, says that the definition of risk in the cognitive neuroscience world is quite similar to the one used in traditional economics. "What we're talking about when we talk about risk are decisions where the outcome is probabilistic—and those probabilities are known," he explains. Yet, unlike the simple economic definition, this "neuroeconomic" one starts to consider people's individual quirks when it comes to risk-taking. It respects that we don't all approach risk the same way.

"Take a roulette wheel, where the odds of winning and losing are known before you make the bet. We all discount probabilistic rewards to some extent: If I give you a gamble where you could get $10 or $12, but the odds of you getting $10 is 100 percent and the odds of you getting $12 is 1 percent, almost everyone will take the first bet," says Buckholtz. "But tolerance for risk differs dramatically between people. If the gamble is between $10 at 100 percent and $1,000 at 30 percent, some people will take the sure bet, and others will take the risky one. So, under conditions of risk, decisions are made by comparing the subjective value of the available decisions, which takes into account the magnitude of gain or loss, the known probability of that outcome, and some individual-specific discounting factor."

Even as the economic definition of risk is extended to consider that "individual-specific discounting factor," it remains logical enough for a man like King to appreciate. Risk remains the probability of a particular outcome—something that we approach with rational analysis. But the cognitive neuroscientists in this field (sometimes referred to as "neuroeconomists") have added an important insight to that very basic economic definition. They appreciate that we humans all approach risk a little bit differently. And, as such, my calculation of a particular probability for the "knowns" of a given decision may be quite different from yours.

Despite this expanded definition, a few issues remain. Most of the decisions we make in our lives don't involve windfalls, coin flips, or roulette wheels. Most of our decisions, in the real world, have to be undertaken without understanding all the probabilities and potential outcomes. Most won't involve a clear choice between a known or an uncertain result. And, as much as we'd like to believe otherwise, humans aren't always rational beings. So, even if we all used something like King's statistical approach to decision-making— which, let's face it, most of us don't—it's doubtful we would ever be able to pin down the probabilities of all potential outcomes, known or not, for a given decision. There are simply too many variables in real life. And more important, we may not know, when it comes time to place our bets, just what all those potential outcomes could be.

Given that the traditional economic definition of risk, even when expanded by cognitive neuroscientists, doesn't appear to work so well outside the laboratory, how might we extend it to fit better in the real world? When I ask my friends to help me define risk, I get a variety of responses. The vast majority are quite specific. Some tend toward the negative, telling me that risk is "scary," "ambiguous," "dangerous," and "a situation where you can't figure out where you'll end up." It's a "gamble" or a "stupid choice." A few others take a more positive tack. They say risk is "exciting," "feeling alive," and "doing something without knowing what will happen next."

Obviously, to some extent, risk is in the eye of the beholder. How you perceive risk is dependent on your experience, your values, and whether or not you happen to have a yen for motocross racing. Hence, Buckholtz's use of terms like "subjective value" and "individual-specific discounting factor." Our own unique and personal perceptions are critical variables that influence us when it comes time to make a risky decision—and they often mean all the difference in whether we decide to push forward or to pull back.

Yet, positive or negative, specific or broad, general or personal, the one thing all these definitions of risk have in common is the idea of uncertainty. Unlike your more traditional definition of risk, which focuses on the known probabilities, people in the real world tend to see risk as something in which we are unsure of the consequences of our behavior, in which the end result of a particular action is something we can't (and perhaps don't want to) know.

As it turns out, scientists don't even agree on a strict definition of risk or risk-taking. As the study of risk has moved out of the economic sphere, picked up by clinical psychologists, epidemiologists, and others, it has been extended in different ways. Marvin Zuckerman, a pioneering personality psychologist who has been studying sensation-seekers, those who seek out new experiences just for the thrill of it, defined risk-taking as "the appraised likelihood of a negative outcome for behavior." Others describe risk as a behavior that carries "potential for harm." And others talk about it as something that ultimately leads to danger, injury, disease, or death. More often than not, economists and cognitive neuroscientists are focused on how individuals calculate the value of the different variables used in the risk-taking equation—while many other scientists are more interested in determining (or preventing) any potential negative outcomes that may be a consequence of that calculation.

Even a single scientist can feel divided on sticking to a definition. When I query Jeff Cooper, a former decision neuroscientist from the California Institute of Technology who has now moved on to the corporate sector, on his own definition of risk, he pauses for a moment.

"The doctrinaire, annoying-scientist part of me would say that any decision where the outcome isn't 100 percent certain is taking a risk—so any decision is risk-taking. Things we call risky decisions are different from safe decisions only by degrees,'" he tells me. "The regular-person side of me would say that risk-taking is making a choice for which the outcome has a reasonable chance of being pretty bad. We think of risk-taking as dangerous—real danger means some real outcome and some plausible chance you might see it."

He raises a good point. Even if we listen to the good scientists and stick to the most basic definition, understanding risk doesn't seem to give us much if it's not grounded in some kind of realistic scenario. What good are calculations if we can't apply them in the real world? It's a valid question—and one that many neuroscientists themselves are asking. In a recent article in the journal *Trends in Cognitive Sciences,* Tom Schonberg, a postdoctoral fellow at the University of Texas at Austin, calls for future studies to "bridge the gap" between economic and more naturalistic risk-taking—and for the creation of experiments that really tap into risky behavior outside gambling tasks. His UT colleague Sarah Helfinstein agrees with him.

"Defining risk as simple outcome variance, which is the way that economists define risk, doesn't work so well in the real world. It's not the way most people think of what risk-taking is, especially when you start talking about taking drugs or having unprotected sex," she explains. "But many neuroscientists still use the economic definition because it's very quantifiable. It's very mathy and, as scientists, we like mathy—but it raises the question of whether we're measuring what we think we're measuring. Or, at least, what the average person thinks we should be measuring."

Mathy is all well and good—and you know that scientists, as well as folks like King love it, but with all this disagreement over a simple definition, how can us regular folks ever hope to gain enough understanding of risk so we can make better decisions? How can we gather the requisite knowledge so we know what risks are worth taking—and what risks we should avoid at any cost?

AN EVERYDAY KIND OF DEFINITION

Perhaps it's time to talk about what the average person thinks we should be measuring when it comes to risk. So, as I try to figure out how to become a smarter risk-taker in my own life, it's clear that a more everyday kind of definition is required. Taking into account what I've heard from scientists, friends, and the risk-takers I know and love, I'm going with this: Risk is a decision or behavior that has a significant probability of resulting in a negative outcome. It's not knowing whether that hand of blackjack will cost you too much of your paycheck, whether your request for a raise will annoy your boss to the point of getting you assigned to that super-demanding client, or whether your parachute will open as advertised on your next skydive. It is part and parcel of every single decision you make, every single day—from what to eat for breakfast to whether to accept that marriage proposal. After all, very few decisions we make in life come with any guarantees. Life is inherently risky.

Needless to say, the math does matter at some level. As we go through life making these decisions, our brains are constantly in a state of calculation: measuring (and often adjusting) the probabilities of various outcomes for a decision and then pushing us toward the choice, barring factors outside our control, that will bring us the most benefit with the least cost. The economists were right about one thing: Risk is a calculation. But it isn't a simple one. And it's not always rational either. Let's go back to Gayle King, our risk-averse number cruncher. I've already told you that he is methodical and disciplined. He'll tell you that he puts enormous faith in the statistics. Even when he hits the casino.

Yes, King, the same man who ultimately chose his career because he could chart his salary progression from numbers published in the back of a magazine, appreciates a good gamble every now and again—even though he knows it's a losing proposition. Yet he does not approach the tables like your stereotypical casino-goer. Once again, he relies on the numbers and considers his actions as part of a larger game of chance. In fact, early on in the days of computers, he worked out his own calculations for many casino games, including the probabilities for all possible blackjack options. He even went so far as to consider the different rules employed by various casinos as he did so. He is nothing if not thorough. He takes me through some of those calculations.

"Blackjack usually has the best odds, with a return over 99 percent of money bet with best statistical play. With rules most favorable to the player, returns can exceed 99.5 percent," he tells me, absentmindedly smoothing his salt-and-pepper mustache with his fingers. He can also (and does) easily rattle off the particular probabilities he calculated for craps (84 to 99.4 percent), poker slots (95 percent), and keno (60 to 65 percent). Still, he concedes that, no matter what game you play, the house always wins. "With good odds, you can play longer and win more often, but one always loses over the long haul," he explains with a sigh. "That's the bad part."

As I said before, from a distance, King might look like the kind of man who avoids risk at all costs. Or, at the very least, one who uses the numbers to find a way minimize it   or to make it work to his advantage. But when I ask him about his favorite game, I learn that he's a big fan of craps, a dice game. Oddly enough, this natural statistician's game of choice is not the one with the best odds. For such an overanalytical guy, this surprises me.

"I like the camaraderie," he says with a bit of a sheepish smile. "It's a lot of fun to be winning when everyone around you is winning at the same time. It's something I really enjoy."

Here we have a case where King knows the numbers. He knows the house always wins—eventually. Yet he goes to the casino anyway, even understanding that the odds are against him. He knows that blackjack ultimately gives you the most bang for your proverbial buck. But when he plays, he doesn't gravitate toward the game with the highest probability for winning. Instead, he sidles up to the craps table, lays down his money, and enthusiastically rolls those dice to the cheers of a crowd, despite the fact that the numbers aren't in his favor.

"I guess I get the same kind of high that someone might get from bungee jumping from an extended roll at the craps table," he tells me with a chuckle. Even your overanalytical, more risk-averse decision-makers can find themselves inspired by more than just the numbers when you put them in the right situation.

That's the thing: We can discuss the odds all day long. We can break down every decision into an equation, some number sentence that describes a thorough calculation of expected probabilities. But by doing so, we leave out some pretty important aspects of the story. The numbers don't tell us how your experience with the game may change the way you play. The numbers don't tell us how it feels to throw the dice with a dozen people not only cheering you on but also raking in the wins right alongside you. The numbers don't tell us how a streak can drum up your confidence. The numbers don't tell us about the stress or emotion involved and how they may affect play. And, finally, the numbers don't tell us about that high, all the fun involved with playing a game—even when you know that you are eventually going to lose.

So, as useful as the numbers might be, they aren't guaranteed to help you make the smartest decisions under risk. Take my boyfriend's unexpected marriage proposal. According to the *Time* magazine article "Why Second Marriages Are More Perilous," I am well within my rights to be wary of a second trip down the aisle. It would appear we don't learn much from the failures in our first marriages. The National Stepfamily Resource Center tells me that 15 percent of remarriages won't last three years. And even if we can stick it out for longer, 39 percent of remarriages fall apart before the ten-year mark. It's not exactly the stuff of hope and encouragement.

Other research, however, says that I'm better off getting remarried. I will be healthier, happier and more financially secure with a partner, even if it is my second time at the rodeo, rather than trying to face the world alone. That makes me feel a little better.

I could compare and contrast the numbers involved with both scenarios to try to make a statistically sound decision. (Though, admittedly, I'm not exactly sure how to create that particular equation—I might have to ask King to set it up on the computer for me, and I have a feeling that he'd be more than happy to do so.) But the stats, good or bad, don't convey a lot of important information that is relevant to my decision. They don't tell you how good my man looks in a suit. They don't tell you what an amazing father he is—or how quickly and easily he has connected with my son. They don't tell you about how damn funny he is, or that we can talk for hours about, well, nothing much at all. They don't tell you how much I miss him when we can't make our schedules sync—or about how my heart has literally skipped a beat when I've caught a glimpse of him across a room. And they don't say much about our shared values and goals. Simply, the numbers don't tell you much about us—or what happens to work for us as a couple. So, while I can keep both the scary and the reassuring numbers in the back of my mind as I consider jumping the broom, I am well aware that they leave out some pretty important aspects of the story.

It would be nice to think that the neuroeconomists are right. That it's all about the calculation. That we humans are rational beings and we are capable of managing risks in a manner that is always to our benefit. But a simple glance at the daily local newspaper, which, on any given day, highlights the varied and often alarming consequences of bad judgment, tells you that simply isn't the case. Even King, a man who is driven by rationality, strays from logic when it comes time to make risky decisions at the casino. We—all of us—want to make the most of risk. We want to find a way to leverage risk so we can capture success and happiness in life. But if we aren't always rational, is there even hope that we can ever learn to do so?

THE GOOD, THE BAD, AND THE UGLY

Now that we've hammered away at the definition, there's another aspect we should discuss: the tone. All this talk about injury, financial loss, and doomed relationships ends up sounding, well, kind of terrifying. Certainly, most things that have the potential to lead to danger, injury, disease, or death don't appear to be in one's best interest, even when discussed in the abstract. When I mention the idea of risk as a negative to Cooper, the former Caltech neuroscientist, he laughs and tells me that risk-taking is a term with a lot of "emotional baggage."

"It's a term that has a real negative valence to it for a lot of people," he says. "Much of that comes from the early studies concerning risk in economic and business schools. The whole idea, back then, in business decision-making was always to minimize risk. So, once people started studying risk in other domains, it was just taken as a given that you want to minimize risk and maximize certainty. That was the formula one needed to follow in order to make optimal decisions."

The conventional concept of risk brings with it a pervasive notion that it's something best avoided. Business executives want to learn more so they can moderate risk and protect their companies' bottom line. Parents, teachers, and legislators want to prevent risky business so that their teenagers can thrive (and survive) into adulthood. Epidemiologists want to minimize the reach of fast-spreading diseases like gonorrhea and measles. The criminal justice system would like to help at-risk youth, not to mention the formerly incarcerated, stay on the straight and narrow. Financiers would like to hold risk at bay and avoid large-scale financial crises. Different aspects of risk are highly correlated with addiction and neuropsychiatric disorders—which, I'm sure, most of us would rather avoid too. And I think just about everyone wants to minimize any unnecessary injury or death.

You can't help seeing the trend here. No matter how you define risk, a lot of the talk will leave you feeling like the world might be better off if people never left their comfort zones. Or their houses, for that matter. Risk is dangerous. Risk is pathological. Risk is just plain *bad*.

Of course, that's not the only way we, as a society, characterize risk. If we look to literature, movies, and popular culture, risk is often described in a tremendously positive manner. Risk-takers are real world supermen (and superwomen)—they are our most beloved celebrities and heroes. When we talk about prosperous risk-takers, we appreciate all they've accomplished despite the potential negatives. Moreover, we often think the fact that they were able to face such peril is a big part of what led to their success.

Stories as old as time have led us to believe that those of us who are willing to take risks—albeit those of the smart, calculated variety—are the ones who will achieve the most in life. Risk-takers get the money, the girl (or boy), the prestige, and the good life. There's a reason why we toss around clichés like "high risk, high reward," "no pain, no gain," and "he who dares wins"—and it's because we're told, time and time again, that throwing caution to the wind is often the only way to make our dreams come true.

There's no way around it: We talk about risk in contradictory extremes. Risk is bad. It can lead to danger and death. Risk is good. It can lead to glory and happiness. So which is it? And how can we make sense of these contradictions so we can better manage risk in our own lives?

As I've said, I want to better understand what risks are worth taking—no, I *need* to better understand what risks are worth taking. And, to do that, I think it's time to strip away the stories, dump the emotional baggage and focus on the facts. I could listen to myths and fairy tales all day. But, as entertaining as they are, they aren't going to help me make my own risk calculations—and make them to my best benefit. They won't explain how the human brain gauges the probabilities of known (and unknown) outcomes—and then determines what risks should be taken. They offer nothing about how much of risk-taking is influenced by our very natures, our personal legacy of genes and biology. And they don't tell us much about how the environment might change the way we calculate risks either.

I'm ready to consider risk beyond the coin flip. I want to know how my DNA might be influencing my decision-making—and just how much weight it really carries when I'm faced with uncertainty. I'd like to know more about how my sex or my gender might be skewing my risk calculations, for better or worse. I want to investigate what environmental factors may be pulling me toward certain kinds of risky behaviors—while pushing me away from others. And I'm sure most of us would also like to better understand how to manage emotion, stress, and errors while we're trying to make smarter decisions.

Life is full of risky propositions. Choose wisely and success awaits. Choose unwisely and, well, the consequences may be too dire to bear. I want to leverage risk in my own life to achieve my goals. And, admittedly, I'd like to keep a modicum of stability in the process. I now have a definition for risk—but no direction on how to better vet it. But, as I said, there are lessons to be learned at the intersection of the laboratory and the real world

And I'm ready to start taking notes. So, to start, let's see what science and successful risk-takers have to say about the role Mother Nature plays when it comes to risk—and whether some of us just inherently possess a better sense of how to manage it in day-to-day life.

PART II

NATURAL-BORN RISK-TAKERS

A FEW YEARS AGO, I WATCHED a television program about Gerlinde Kaltenbrunner, the first female mountaineer to summit all eight of the world's tallest mountains without the use of supplemental oxygen. For many who climb these majestic yet perilous peaks, that extra oxygen is a vital accessory. Without it, the thinner atmosphere at extreme altitudes can really mess with a body, causing physical and mental exhaustion. Symptoms of altitude sickness include shortness of breath, increased heart rate, dizziness, and cognitive impairment. Some people have even reported hallucinations. So, as you might imagine, when you need every available physical and mental resource to struggle to the top of these mountains, not having extra oxygen significantly increases your risk of injury or death. In fact, a study out of the University of Washington found that even experienced mountaineers were three times more likely to die trying to summit Mount Everest without it.

But some climbers don't (read: won't) use supplemental oxygen. When Kaltenbrunner was asked about her decision not to use it during this program, I remember thinking she seemed almost glib as she explained her choice. She said it just wasn't something she wanted to do—for her, there was joy in climbing with only the bare essentials. And this really surprised me. Perhaps it was because Kaltenbrunner didn't quite fit my image of the risk-taking daredevil type. With her bright eyes and warm smile, she looked like someone I might run into at a yoga class or in the after-school pickup line—not like some outdoorsy thrill-seeker who could so easily throw caution to the wind.

Years later, thinking back on that show, I have to wonder how glib she really was (or is, as she is still an active climber) about the risks involved with her decision to climb without that oh-so-important oxygen. I'm sure she has a good handle on both the dangers involved in her sport and her own physical capabilities. But, at the time, as suburban as she might look from the outside, Kaltenbrunner appeared almost superhuman to me. She seemed like someone whose body and mind didn't need the same supports or comforts that mine would when faced with a challenge. And this went beyond her oxygen choices; her decision to pursue mountaineering full-time, with its harsh physical demands, grueling cold, and physical dangers, also appeared risky to me. Too damn risky, in fact. A woman like that, I thought, must be wired differently than I am. And such profound differences would have to be innate—present since, if not before, birth.

Some have argued that risk-takers are born, not made. There is something in their very nature that allows them to approach the world in a unique fashion—and that approach is part and parcel of their success. They are hardwired to handle risk, constructed from different biological building blocks than the rest of us. And while we can always watch them in awe, we'd have little luck in trying to emulate their behavior. We tend to believe that those kinds of risk-takers—individuals like Kaltenbrunner—act largely from instinct, directed by unique variations in their genes, brain circuits, and bodies. I doubt I could ever attempt to mimic Kaltenbrunner's feats, with or without oxygen. To be honest, I don't think I would ever seriously consider trying to.

When you look at someone like Kaltenbrunner—or any other prolific risk-taker, for that matter—the "born, not made" explanation feels true. But does such an argument hold water? Are successful risk-takers really built all that differently from the rest of us mere mortals? As it turns out, scientists are learning quite a bit about how our brains, our genes, our genders, and our ages influence how we perceive and pursue risks. And those differences are helping to explain why some of us tend to be natural-born risk-takers while others instinctively shy away from danger and uncertainty.

Chapter Three

RISK AND THE BRAIN

MICHELLE STARTED HER software development career during the 1990s dot-com explosion. Straight out of college, she picked up a job with a small Internet security start-up. She loved working for such a young, vibrant company—it had the kind of passionate (and irreverent) environment that made each day's work a lot of fun. And she adored her colleagues there too. They not only worked together, but they played together. A lot. Sometimes, she admits, it felt more like some kind of a social club than an actual professional gig. But the group had a kind of shared mission and camaraderie that blew Michelle away. Taken together, it was everything a job *should* be.

"It was a really good time. Looking back, I'm not sure how we got any work done," she says, laughing. "But we did. And it was good work. It meant something—and, together, we were able to create things that were really innovative and different."

Michelle stayed on with the company as it steadily grew and was then acquired by a large international software services corporation—a move that changed nearly everything about her beloved workplace, from the way they did business to the people they employed. She found that day-to-day life on the job also dramatically altered. She had to say goodbye to many longtime friends and colleagues as they were transferred elsewhere (or, too often, branded redundant and laid off). She had to let go of a more unorthodox situation and get accustomed to a very traditional corporate environment. She had to start filling out time sheets, sending formatted memos, and learning new business processes. She had to learn to dress like a businessperson instead of a college student. And, as she tried to adapt to all those new changes, Michelle realized just what an uncommon and marvelous experience her start-up job had been.

Michelle admits she was one of the lucky ones. By the time the dot-com industry imploded, and many of her friends were out of work, she had a solid, reliable gig and the possibility to move up the ladder with a large corporation. Her stock options didn't vanish into the ether, unlike those of so many other people who worked for start-ups during that time. Instead, thanks to the acquisition, her stock provided enough to put a substantial down payment on a beautiful home. Today, she has adjusted to the more regimented environment of this corporate Goliath and has risen in the ranks too—but she acutely misses those halcyon start-up days.

"It's a good job. I shouldn't complain. But it's just not that much fun," she says with a shrug. "Work really is *work* now."

When I ask Michelle if she would ever go back to a start-up environment, she is circumspect. "If it were the right opportunity, I'd certainly consider it. But as much as I am all 'glory days' about my start-up life, it would be hard to leave," she says of her current job. "I am paid really well. I have great benefits. I'm settled here. And, as much as anyone can have job security, I have it. Leaving would be a big risk. But it's a lot of fun to dream about."

A few weeks later, after a call from one of her former start-up colleagues about a potential job with a new company, Michelle finds herself considering that risk. The opportunity sounds ideal—and a hell of a lot of fun. She could reconnect with old colleagues, trade in those sensible business suits for blue jeans, and maybe, just maybe, feel excited about work again. And she'd get a slight pay raise too. But there would be substantial trade-offs. She'd have to take a cut in some of her benefits. The decrease in vacation time, she tells me, is particularly painful to consider. And, in addition to all that, she'd have to pick up and move halfway across the country to Austin, Texas, taking her away from longtime friends and her extended family. It is a big risk. But, she admits, it's also quite a compelling one.

Should Michelle stay at the safe, well-paid job that bores her? Or should she leave and enter an entirely new professional and personal situation to see whether she can recapture some of that start-up magic? How will she determine the risks involved with this decision? Like any of us considering taking a risk, she'll rely on a variety of physiological systems, including a specific circuit hidden within the very recesses of our brains, to help her determine whether she should make the jump or stay put.

OUR RISK CIRCUITRY

....

That specific circuit is the mesocortical limbic pathway, which, as noted, is often referred to as the brain's "reward" processing circuit. And it does play a critical role in helping us process rewards. But since no reward comes without some risk, as Craig Ferris, neuroscientist at Northeastern, puts it, the mesocortical limbic pathway is really like the brain's motivation system, a circuit involved with evaluating both the risks and rewards involved with any decision. It's the part of the brain responsible for calculating predictability: If I engage in this behavior, just what might be the result?

The mesocortical limbic circuit is made up of three key brain systems: the basal ganglia, a cluster of regions near the brain stem that focuses on food, sex, social behaviors, and other key rewards; the prefrontal cortex, the brain's executive control center; and the limbic system, the seat of emotion and memory. This important pathway is what helps us make decisions as we go about our day. And each individual system in it does its part by providing the specific information your brain requires to successfully perceive, process, and pursue risk.

Basal Ganglia

Nestled deep inside our skulls, underneath the cortex, are the basal ganglia, which make up our so-called reptilian brain. Millions and millions of years ago, water creatures crawled up from the depths to try their luck on dry land. Scientists believe those far-off evolutionary ancestors had brains that looked remarkably like the subcortical brain areas you and I have in our own heads. And certainly, the basal ganglia look and work just about the same in today's reptiles, birds, mammals, primates, humans.

The basal ganglia are not one brain region, but rather a collection of several different areas that make a functional brain unit. Hence the name: basal, for being located near the base of the brain; and ganglia, for structures containing neurons. Unless you are a hard-

BASAL GANGLIA

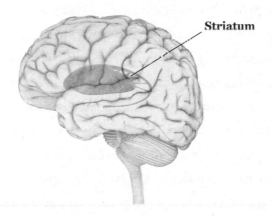

Striatum

core anatomy buff, you might not be able to distinguish one bit from the next. Still, each component plays a unique role in influencing our choices.

The largest region is the corpus striatum, often just called the striatum. It's known for its striped appearance and houses smaller subregions like the caudate nucleus, the putamen, and the nucleus accumbens. Nearby, the pale globe of the pallidum, the globus pallidus, and the ventral pallidum take up residence. Adjacent, the mysterious "black substance," or substantia nigra, stands out from the crowd with its dark coloring. The ventral tegmental area and subthalamic nucleus, a small bit next to the thalamus, round out the mix. Together, they play an important role in helping us make decisions.

Our reptilian brain has been linked to our most base desires—food, drink, sex, companionship, money, and social status. Simply stated, this region helps motivate us to go after life's best rewards. Which, when you think about it, are the very things for which we are willing to take the most risks as we go about our business. So, it makes sense that you'll find the basal ganglia at the center of our risk-and-reward-processing pathway.

By representing those things we want the most in life, the basal ganglia hold considerable sway over almost every aspect of cognition—including decision-making. Therefore, these systems come online rapidly. Some scientists would even go so far as to say they come online automatically. This is part of what Daniel Kahneman, in his book *Thinking, Fast and Slow*, calls the fast-thinking system. And given its focus on all those base desires, a slower, more deliberate system that could help override quick, reward-based decisions when necessary would be a good thing to have around too.

Prefrontal Cortex

Let's face it: Making decisions based on the value of rewards alone is hardly sound. Can you imagine if all our choices were based on only what we wanted at the present moment? If we were solely driven by food, sex, money, or other forms of immediate personal gain, the world would be a pretty unproductive—not to mention a pretty inhospitable—place. To exist in a civilized society, we need to have a way to control ourselves even when the most tempting of treats are within reach. We need the power of "no"—or, at least, "not now." And so, the slower-working, more rational areas of the brain help keep the basal ganglia in check.

As the human species evolved, we developed the large neocortex that differentiates us from lower-order mammals. Our hefty frontal lobes, the largest part of the brain, helm that larger, more evolved

PREFRONTAL CORTEX

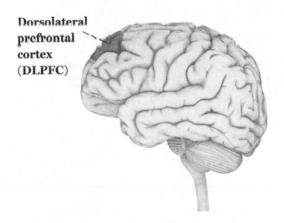

Dorsolateral prefrontal cortex (DLPFC)

system. And the prefrontal cortex, the frontmost part of the frontal lobe, is the brain region implicated in judgment, reasoning, and inhibition. This is the area of the brain that helps us to think before we act, so to speak. To put on the brakes before we do ourselves, or someone else, harm. The frontal cortex, in Kahneman's language, is the slow-thinking system.

The frontal cortex and basal ganglia are permanently coupled, communicating through strong neural connections that pass information to and from both regions. Different parts of the basal ganglia link up with specific parts of the prefrontal cortex, like the dorsolateral prefrontal cortex (DLPFC). Located on the top of the frontal lobe, the DLPFC is important in decision-making; patients with damage to the DLPFC have great difficulty making decisions. And research suggests that the DLPFC helps us stay in control as we respond to the environment around us. It works as the brain's regulator, inhibiting impulsive behaviors that may not be acceptable to exhibit.

Joshua Buckholtz, the Harvard neuroscientist, likens the basal ganglia–prefrontal cortex stretch of the circuit (sometimes referred to as the fronto-striatal loop) to the brain's "gas" and "brakes." The striatum, part of the basal ganglia, encodes the value of the reward. That's the gas, the impulse and motivation to go after the things you want. But the gas should never be left completely unchecked—that's how you crash and burn. So the frontal lobes, particularly the DLPFC, act as the brakes. But since DLPFC is a bit of a mouthful, we can just call it the "regulator." And this regulator can tap the brakes by directly inhibiting behaviors that might not be in your best interest or by modifying how the striatum encodes value, pushing the basal ganglia to include things like long-term goals and consequences when calculating the value of different options.

This particular loop in the circuit is important to making smart decisions. But the mesocortical limbic pathway doesn't end there. It couldn't. We require an important third input to help improve our decision-making capabilities. An important input that adds experience and emotion to the mix.

Limbic System

Cue the brain's limbic system. The basal ganglia are linked to a second part of the prefrontal cortex, an area known as the ventromedial prefrontal cortex, or VMPFC (it's tucked on the underside of the frontal lobe, close to the eyes), which then links up with the brain's emotional processing region, better known as the limbic system.

The limbic system includes several key brain areas, including the hippocampus, the brain's memory epicenter; the amygdala, known best for its instant situational assessments, including the hearty fight-or-flight response; the cingulate gyrus, the part of the cortex that associates rewards and actions to help us learn from past experience; and the insula, the part of the brain thought to help regulate emotion. The limbic system ties both emotion and experience into your decisions, so you can apply what you've learned from similar situations in the past to help you out in present. It enables you to compute and represent the subjective value of the potential reward, based on what's important to you,

LIMBIC SYSTEM

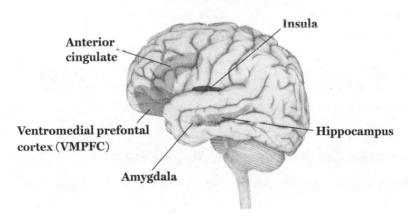

Insula

Anterior cingulate

Ventromedial prefontal cortex (VMPFC)

Hippocampus

Amygdala

and then sends that information on up to the prefrontal cortex. Simply stated, the VMPFC is a calculator. It integrates all that personal and experiential data, uniting information from emotion, memory, and environment, so you can better determine whether stepping on the gas or pumping the brakes will bring you a more optimal outcome.

MESOCORTICAL LIMBIC CIRCUITRY

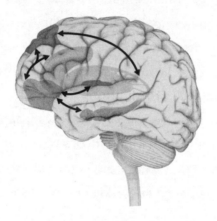

THREE SYSTEMS, ONE CIRCUIT, LOTS OF LEARNING

These three systems—the basal ganglia, prefrontal cortex, and the limbic system—together form the complete mesocortical limbic circuit. Simply stated, it's a probability computer. It's a sophisticated brain system uniquely designed to help us process not only the potential and personally adjusted rewards that may await us if we make a particular decision but also the potential risks inherent to that choice—and, with luck, guide us to the best judgment for the situation at hand.

Over time, those judgments help us gain valuable experience. In fact, scientists argue that risky decisions may actually help us learn faster and more efficiently. Why might that be? It comes down to dopamine.

You've likely heard about dopamine—one of the most widely studied neurotransmitters in the nervous system. In popular science news, dopamine is linked to all manner of things, including sex, schizophrenia, infidelity, motivation, addiction, attention, learning, lactation, gambling, overeating, attention-deficit/hyperactivity disorder, exploration, politics, love, Parkinson's disease, movement, obsessive-compulsive disorder, and social media use—and that's just to name a few. It also helps to fuel the mesocortical limbic circuit. So, it's a neurochemical that has some serious reach, assisting with complex cognitive processes like learning, memory, and movement.

Decades ago, researchers thought that dopamine worked solely by way of pleasure. You had some sex, ate something yummy, or got hold of some other rewarding item, and dopamine surged out of the basal ganglia in response. That release facilitated learning, priming the brain to help you do whatever might be needed to get your hands on that reward again. It turns out that the truth is a little more subtle. Dopamine is certainly released in response to reward, but the amount released depends heavily on expectation.

Michael Frank, a neuroscientist at Brown University, studies how basal ganglia influence decision-making. He says that dopamine is a big facilitator of learning. After all, rewards are great. When you get something good, it pays to figure out how you managed it so that you can get it again. And again. And maybe a few more times after that—especially if the reward is particularly enticing. And that's just what lab rats, having learned to associate a lever with something good, will do.

Rats can be very easily trained to associate a reward with a paired stimulus—usually, a lever press that results in a sugar pellet, a little fruit juice, or perhaps a nice, stimulating hit of cocaine. The animal will often wander around its enclosure for a bit, accidentally stumble on that lever, and thus receive a treat. This, of course, inspires the rat to go back to try its luck with the lever again, helping the rat learn to link the stimulus (the lever press) with that cool reward.

"The basal ganglia circuit is perfectly structured to help execute reward-based learning," Frank tells me. "It allows you to learn about positive and negative outcomes of your choices. When you have that increase in dopamine, you are more likely to pursue the same rewarding outcome in the future."

It would be easy to think that it's simply the reward that's driving this learning process. After all, who doesn't want some more sugar? But there's more to it than that. Certainly, a plain old reward does result in the release of some dopamine. But Frank has found that an unexpected reward results in a deluge of this neurotransmitter. That nice reward-based learning that our friendly rat so nicely demonstrated for us? Well, it happened because those first few rewards were so unexpected. That rush of dopamine from the unexpected facilitates neuroplasticity, or changes to the brain circuitry, helping the animal to make the connection between "press lever" and "get the good stuff." And once the connection is there, the animal will keep on pressing.

But here's the thing: Over time, even as that newly learned lever-pressing behavior becomes a habit, less and less dopamine will be released in response to the reward. So, while we are quick to talk about reward-based learning, we might be better off calling it "unexpected-reward-based learning"—because it's the unexpected that reaps the most dopamine and gets that critical learning process started. Expected rewards don't work the same kind of magic—or result in that same amount of dopamine being released.

Of course, our reptilian brain isn't all about the rewards. It also processes negative consequences—after all, if human beings focused only on the positive, we'd be pretty easy pickings out there in the world. Humans need to deal with negative stimuli too, so we can learn what to avoid in life. So let's switch up the rat's lever scenario. Now when the animal gives it a pull, it receives a rather nasty electric shock. Now you'll find that dopamine works in a different fashion. Neuroscientists have observed that this negative consequence turns the dopamine release nearly off. And in doing so, it helps the animal learn to avoid the bad lever in the future.

You see the same thing in human beings when dopamine is tracked using neuroimaging techniques. The unexpected and positive results in a huge hit of dopamine, influencing the entire mesocortical limbic circuitry. Negative stimuli all but dry up the dopamine well. And expected rewards? Well, they are good—but they just don't result in the same kind of dopamine surge as unexpected rewards do. They elicit more of a dopamine trickle.

Why is this important? When you get that extra boost of dopamine from an unanticipated reward—from taking a risk and having it work out in your favor—it results in a neurobiological advantage that can help you learn.

"Sticking with the status quo can make it hard to learn and improve at anything. Say you decide that you want to learn how to rock climb. So you go to a climbing wall and decide to try the easiest course there," Frank explains. "But let's say you soon find out that the easiest level is really quite easy, even for a beginner, and you achieve it. If you don't rely on risk and try a harder course the next time, you're never going to become a better rock climber."

It makes sense. If you don't take a risk, you won't get that extra hit of dopamine to help push those learning signals. If you never get off the easy climbing course and push yourself a bit, you'll never improve your skills. If you don't get up the gumption to talk to that hot chick at the bar, she's never going to have your babies. If you stay at your boring corporate gig, you may miss out on an amazing new professional opportunity.

"When you're in a situation with risk, the learning signals in your brain are stronger," Frank says—and his laboratory work certainly backs up that statement. "The way in which people get better at things, at anything, is to take some risks and constantly change the level of expectation."

There's not a lot of the unexpected to be found in Michelle's current position. She's kind of bored with the day-to-day—and she'll be the first to admit that she is not learning much. She has no idea what to expect from the new start-up. And the risks involved in not knowing make it a unique opportunity for her to learn some new skills. The kind of new skills, perhaps, that could help her succeed in all manner of future gigs.

THE ANATOMY OF A DECISION

Michelle has quite a bit to consider as she makes this decision. So, what is happening in her brain as she tries to decide? Well, from what neuroscientists have pieced together so far, it would seem that the mesocortical limbic circuit, working with some other key brain areas, uses those important dopamine signals to calculate outcome probabilities to predict subjective value and maximize utility. That is, when faced with a decision, the brain computes the probabilities of potential outcomes by gathering information from both the current environment and our past experiences about each choice, and then weighting each alternative with a subjective value based on our needs, wants, beliefs, and goals. The idea is that by taking all these variables into account, we can make sensible choices that will help us further our goals (that being the utility bit)—and ultimately survive and, with luck, thrive.

Sounds remarkably rational, no? That's the assumption, at any rate. Jeff Cooper, the former Caltech neuroscientist who now works in the corporate world, likens the decision-making regions of the brain to one big numbers game, regardless of whether we're making choices about love, food, poker, or life in general. "It's all numbers up here at some point," he tells me, tapping the front of his head to indicate the brain. "Everything."

Even when you consider that we are not always rational decision-makers, the idea that the mesocortical limbic circuit guides our choices makes a fair bit of sense. The three brain systems provide key information about our decision. The basal ganglia represent our needs and our desires. The limbic system gives input about our emotions and our past experiences. Rounding out the mix is the prefrontal cortex, which offers us reason and executive control. And by yoking these three key systems together, we should enough information we need to make the best possible decision.

Let's consider Michelle's situation. She has just been offered a compelling and more lucrative job by a former trusted colleague. It sounds like an interesting gig—with a lot of fun people. And the idea of leaving a more traditional corporate environment to do something new and exciting, especially given Michelle's previous experience with a start-up, is something—to use Joshua Buckholtz's metaphor—that gives her a good bit of gas. These benefits offer the kind of motivation that is hard to resist. Her reptilian brain is all aflutter with the possibilities (and a fair bit of dopamine).

Yet Michelle already has a damn good job, complete with a good salary, benefits, and job security. She may be a bit bored with her day-to-day work (and is equally bored of corporate fashion requirements), but she doesn't hate coming into work every day. Plus, she's been in the area since college. She has put down roots there—and has an extended support network of friends and family. Taking the job would mean leaving an established position as well as leaving an established social network. So, as she considers the job offer, as tempting as it might be, her more rational prefrontal systems are coming online—and, in response, her mental foot is hovering over the brakes. She needs to adjust and consider what would be best. The new gig sounds really amazing. But it would be a huge change, professionally and personally. Not to mention, it's a start-up. Sure, there's funding now. But will it still be operating in the black next year? In this economy, even with good people at the helm of a new company, it's impossible to know. She may make this big move and then find herself unemployed and alone in Texas. Knowing all this, should she take the job and see if she can't relive those start-up glory days? Or should she play it safe and stay put? Should she pump the gas or hit the brakes?

The basal ganglia play a key role in assessing the value of the reward—the new job. And as Michelle finds herself contemplating pulling on some panty hose and dealing with another day of corporate meetings, the idea of building a new business with a trusted, creative colleague, is quite a prize. Plus, there's a salary upgrade. You can see why a change would be so compelling—leading to an increase of dopamine in the basal ganglia.

In a second, separate pathway, the basal ganglia also represent potential negatives—you know, any negative consequences that may come with making the jump: the loss of a social network, the lack of vacation time, and the fear of the unknown. And, as a result, the initial dopamine surge is flattening out.

The prefrontal system comes online a little slower than the basal ganglia do. But it's pretty busy computing and comparing the subjective probabilities of a successful and fulfilling career if she takes the new job versus the potential outcomes, including, perhaps, a less fulfilling but more secure career path, if she turns it down. As it takes in the information from the reptilian brain, the prefrontal system is simultaneously receiving information from the limbic system. Important data from the brain's memory and information centers need to be considered here, as well. Data that represent the excitement of a new job, the satisfaction Michelle derives from her current position, her memories of how fun start-up work is, thoughts of leaving her local friends and family, and the importance of a good benefits package.

The VMPFC, the prefrontal calculator, in particular, is taking in all this information to compute the subjective value of the job offer, given Michelle's current situation. All three brain systems are sending information back and forth, at incredible speed, encoding information about needs, wants, morals, experience, environment, emotions, and goals, to help her choose the best of her risky options. It's a rather clever arrangement: Our deepest (and fastest) yearnings can be tempered by reason and experience; our more prudent judgments softened by desire and need. It's a potent mix that makes sure we're sufficiently motivated to go after the things we need—and want—the most. But not at a cost that may be too great to bear.

The push and pull of these systems—two quick and instinctual, and the third rational and deliberate—work together to help us make optimal decisions. From a neurobiological perspective, the mesocortical limbic circuit ties longing, reason, and emotion up with one big neurobiological bow, influencing our choices by comparing and contrasting the personal value of a reward with the dangers involved in trying to acquire it. It's the ultimate in brain-based checks and balances.

BREAKING THE CIRCUIT

....

It all sounds so simple. With such a sensible arrangement, we should all be making optimal decisions every single time, right? This brain setup should immediately tell Michelle what she should do—and it should be the best choice available. With such circuitry in place, mistakes should be all but an impossibility. Unfortunately, as with any system of checks and balances, if one segment gets out of whack, the rest of the system suffers.

Think about it: If we place too much weight on our desires, and our basal ganglia rule the day, we probably won't make the best decision. The same is true if the limbic system or the prefrontal cortex has too much sway. After all, being overly emotional or judgmental doesn't help with good decision-making either.

In Michelle's case, if the old colleague who made her the offer was a former mentor, someone she really admired and trusted, she may be more likely to take the job despite the move to Texas and the cut to her benefits. If she focuses too much on the personal costs of moving away from friends and family, she may turn down the job, which may not be the right choice for her career. If she finds herself overthinking the whole situation, letting her prefrontal cortex take her into a vicious cycle of indecisiveness, she may hesitate just long enough for the job offer to disappear into thin air. As you can see, a simple modification to any of the variables in this decision-making equation is likely to change the so-called optimal choice.

But how might the weights of those choices change? Peter Brugger, a neurologist at Switzerland's University Hospital Zurich, devised an experiment to change up the system's checks and balances by noninvasively disrupting the DLPFC, that prefrontal cortex "regulator," during a gambling task using a technique called repetitive transcranial magnetic stimulation (rTMS).

Neurons communicate in the language of electrochemical signals. And scientists have long known how to modulate brain activity using electrical currents. Each neuron has a voltage-dependent membrane that can be amped up or down by the electrical activity of surrounding cells, and you can manipulate neural processing by applying a direct current to the skull. It's the theory behind an overly maligned treatment for depression and other mood disorders: electroshock therapy. Those shocks to the skull can change the electrical communication between neurons, doing wonders for common symptoms of severe depression in the process. But, alas, they also could result in some pretty awful side effects, including seizure, memory loss, and general confusion.

rTMS avoids some of the unpleasantness of electroshock by using a unique magnetic coil to direct brief pulses outside the skull—a method that induces smaller, more controllable electrical currents. Those resulting currents can either heighten or dampen neural activity in specific areas of the cortex for a short period of time, usually on the order of a few milliseconds. I know it still sounds remarkably unpleasant, but as someone who experienced rTMS as a graduate research assistant, I can honestly say that it's not that bad. I wouldn't call being zapped by an rTMS coil the most agreeable feeling in the world. It feels a bit like a small yet sudden rap on the head. But it's more than tolerable. Folks in my department likened each zap of the rTMS to a "brain fart," a quick and temporary duh-type moment that one can easily shake off. But that one little zap to a specific spot can change up some pretty complex behaviors.

Brugger and company used the rTMS coil technique to manip-ulate the DLPFC in a group of young men as they played a com-puterized version of that perennial carny favorite, the shell game. Study participants were presented with six boxes laid out horizon-tally across the screen. Each box could be pink or blue, and the ratio of pink to blue boxes varied from trial to trial. The task itself was fairly simple. Under one of those six boxes was a winning token. Participants just had to guess whether the winning token would be under a pink box or a blue one. If they guessed correctly, they would receive a certain number of points. The number of points received was based directly on the probabilities involved. For example, if five blue boxes and one pink box were on-screen, the lowest risk prospect would be the color blue. If a participant played it safe and selected blue (and the token was actually under a blue box), he'd receive a nominal number of points. If he selected pink, however, and was correct in said guess, he'd get a much richer point reward.

Incorrect choices worked in a similar manner. If he chose the high-risk option and was wrong, he'd lose a higher point value. If he played it safe and lost, he'd lose a few points but not enough to hurt too badly. The goal, for each participant, was to amass the most points he could across 100 different trials.

To explore how a zap to the DLPFC might influence the risk-taking process, Brugger's team zapped nine of the study participants on the right side of the prefrontal cortex and the other nine on the left side of the same region before each made his color choice. This deactivated the DLPFC—which, in turn, reduced the region's regulatory capabilities. The researchers quickly discovered that individuals who received rTMS to the right side of the regulator exhibited much riskier decision-making than those who were zapped on the left side or received no stimulation at all.

The researchers argue that the prefrontal cortex, particularly the regulator, plays an important role in the "suppression of superficially seductive options." And when it is deactivated by an electromagnetic pulse, it can't do its job. This fits right in with Buckholtz's idea of the prefrontal cortex acting as decision-making brakes. When the regulation activity is suppressed, we have a much harder time tempering our choices. We can't suppress enticing options like an exciting gamble on a high-risk game. So, we are much more likely to discount outcome probabilities—to pick pink even when we see five blue boxes on the screen—when there is the possibility of a tempting (and large) reward.

And what happens when you amp up neural activity in the regulator? As you might expect, there's a decrease in risky choices. Alvaro Pascual-Leone, a researcher at the Berenson-Allen Center for Noninvasive Brain Stimulation at Harvard Medical School, and Brugger's co-author on the rTMS study, steered a follow-up study using the same task but a different stimulation technique called transcranial direct current stimulation (tDCS), which sends a low, direct, and constant current through electrodes placed on the scalp. It's perfectly safe—and those little electrodes, though causing a bit of an itchy feeling across the scalp, result in an increase in neural excitability in the brain region underneath.

When individuals received tDCS to the prefrontal regulator before making choices, the increased neural activity resulted in study participants playing it safe. They tended to choose less risky options, in comparison with those who received a sham, or pretend, tDCS zap. With the increased activity to a key part of the brain's brake system, these individuals controlled their behavior to the point that they started to avoid bigger risks. Taken together, these studies demonstrate the importance of the brain's regulator in helping us balance out risks as we make decisions—and just what can happen when there's a break in the mesocortical limbic circuit.

PREDICTING RISK

....

All three systems of the mesocortical limbic pathway play an important role in making good decisions. And by investigating the activity in each, scientists can even predict when you'll take a risk and when you'll play it safe. Sarah Helfinstein, a postdoctoral fellow at the University of Texas at Austin who studies risk-taking, and her colleagues looked at brain activity while participants did something called the Balloon Analog Risk Task (BART). Researchers who study naturalistic risk-taking, such as driving drunk or having unprotected sex, prefer the BART to more traditional neuroeconomic tasks because it is highly correlated with real-world risk-taking behaviors—more of the "should I drive 90 miles per hour even though the speed limit is 45?" type of decisions over the "should I take the guaranteed payout or gamble for a little bit more?"

The task is simple enough. A virtual balloon appears on a screen. By pressing a button, you can pump it up. Each pump gets you a few points, so the more you pump, the higher your score (and, ultimately, the higher monetary reward you will receive). But, as with real balloons, you can take things too far. One pump too many and—*boom!*—the balloon pops. And if the balloon pops, you get nothing. So you have an exit door. You can choose to stop pumping and walk away with the points you've already accrued at any time instead of continuing to pump. It's the safer option. The basic idea here is to pump as many times as you can, accruing as many points as you can, without popping the balloon and losing it all. But how many pumps takes you to the pop is unknown—each one has a randomly set explosion point.

"This is a task that really taps into your general willingness to engage in risk, across a lot of domains," Helfinstein says. "To really maximize your points, you actually have to pump more that most people typically do. You have to behave in a way that's more risky. It's also a task most people really get into. There's a feeling of escalating tension as you play, because you really try to get as many pumps in as you can without popping the balloon."

I can attest to that. Helfinstein was kind enough to let me try my hand at balloon pumping when I visited her at UT Austin. Unlike many of the neuroeconomic tasks I've tried over the course of my research, it's something that can get you going. I mean, really get you going. Over dozens of trials, I found myself perched on the edge of my seat, giving myself mental pats on the back when my pumps upped my points and grimacing in frustration when that stupid balloon popped, leaving me with nothing. While I won't say the thrill is as strong as driving too fast or jumping out of a plane, it is definitely compelling. And as it turns out, in terms of BART results, I'm just a hair more risk-seeking than average. I pump a little more often than your average Joe—meaning I'm a bit more likely to keep pumping than to cash out. Which, according to the research, means I'm a little more open to risky choices than most.

If Helfinstein had put me in a functional magnetic resonance imaging (fMRI) scanner during my visit, she might have been able to predict my BART score just by looking at the activity in my mesocortical limbic circuitry. In a recent study, she and her colleagues recruited 108 participants to have their brains scanned while playing the BART. The researchers then fed the fMRI data from the BART into a computer program and, using a classification algorithm, asked it to try to figure out which brain activity patterns denoted risky choices and which ones were linked to playing it safe. That is, they compared the trials where people continued to pump to those where folks cashed out to see what brain regions were most active.

This program was able to accurately predict participants' decisions based on activity in the prefrontal cortex approximately 70 percent of the time. By looking specifically for activation patterns linked to risky choices, Helfinstein and her colleagues found prefrontal regions, as well as areas in the limbic system like the insula and anterior cortex, were much less active when study participants chose to keep pumping—and much more active when study participants played it safe and chose to cash out. So, if we go back to Buckholtz's analogy, it would seem that people who keep pumping on the BART, acting in a riskier fashion, are simply not engaging the brain's brake system. This, Helfinstein argues, points to the importance of having a strong executive control center when it comes to making good decisions.

RISKY TO GO, RISKY TO STAY

The prefrontal cortex takes in information from the basal ganglia and the limbic system—and then both calculates the potential outcome probabilities and regulates our behaviors. As Michelle tries to make a decision, she is definitely relying on her slower-thinking systems while she considers all her variables. In fact, her prefrontal cortex seems to be putting in overtime. As she tells me about her decision-making process, it's clear that her DLPFC is in fine working order. Though excited about the possibility of a jump, she can't help hovering over the brakes. "It's a risk to go, and it's a risk to stay," she says with an audible sigh. "I'm just trying to figure out which risk will be easier to live with a year from now."

After considering all her options and weighing what's most important to her, she makes a decision. In the end, the move to Texas proves to be too much—despite the promise of extra money. Michelle loves her house, as well as having friends and family close by. Even with a more fun, social work environment, there's no telling how long it might take her to build up that same kind of support network in a new place. And if the company fell apart, as so many new businesses do, after a year or two? She'd feel stranded so far away from home. But that's not the only reason to stay, she admits. She also likes her current benefits package. Sure, the higher salary that she's being offered would be nice. But not as nice as having five weeks of paid vacation a year. So Michelle reluctantly decides to turn down the job offer and stay with her current company.

"It was a good opportunity. But not the perfect opportunity," she explains. "And it would take something pretty near perfect to get me to make a big move at this point."

Michelle's mesocortical limbic circuitry weighed the pros and cons of this particular decision—and opted to pump the brakes. Her basal ganglia and limbic system provided key dopamine signals to the prefrontal cortex based on her wants, her needs, and her past experiences. Her prefrontal system was then able to calculate the subjective value that worked best for her—which, in this case, meant turning down the offer. When push came to shove, Michelle found that friends and family were more important to her than a fun (but somewhat unpredictable) start-up opportunity.

Someone else might have weighted those same variables differently, putting more emphasis on the extra salary or the ability to be in a less stodgy environment, and calculated a different result. They may have simply heard the words, "Austin, Texas," and immediately started pricing moving companies. For each of us, the mesocortical limbic circuit is working as a risk computer, determining what decision will offer us the best chance of success given what we want, what we know, and what's best for our future.

Michelle's tale may seem like more of a story about how to *not* take a risk. After all, in the end, she stayed put. But, really, it was a balanced calculation between two risky choices. As she said, it was a risk to go and it was a risk to stay. But who knows what opportunity might come Michelle's way next? It may involve a more local setting, a little more vacation time, or a more provocative business plan. Over time, the weights of her decision-making variables will change accordingly. With the right variables in place, the mesocortical limbic circuit might calculate out a different decision, one where Michelle can dump her panty hose and ride the start-up wave again.

Chapter Four

....

RISK AND GENES

ANDY FRANKENBERGER DOES NOT like being called a gambler. To some, it may sound like he's quibbling. After all, he was a successful trader of equity derivatives for almost 15 years on Wall Street. And now he's a professional poker player—and a good one at that. Certainly there are those who would tell you that "Wall Street trader" and "poker player" are pretty much synonymous. But gambling, according to Frankenberger, has very little to do with his successes in either field.

"Sure, there's a component of poker that involves putting your money at risk, just as you do when investing or trading stocks," he says. "But, in both, you are making educated decisions about where you want to place your money. The word 'gambling' has the connotation of taking haphazard risk. You're supposed to lose when you go to the casino—over time, the house always wins because the odds are uniformly stacked in their favor. In poker and trading, however, if you have strong analytical skills and a disciplined, rigorous approach to risk management, there's a good chance you are going to win over time."

And win he has. As a newcomer to the poker circuit, Frankenberger was named the 2011 World Poker Tour Player of the Year. After only a few years of tournament play, he has won two World Series of Poker championships. One of those wins, notably, was against Phil Ivey, largely considered the greatest poker player in the world—a man of few words, penetrating stares, and impeccable poker skills.

Somehow, Frankenberger has managed to thrive in not one but two risky careers. And to do so almost immediately after joining both fields. It makes you wonder how he does it. He cites his "disciplined, rigorous approach to risk management." And there's probably something to that. But given his extraordinary successes, I can't help wondering if Frankenberger's approach has more to do with innate proficiencies over learned skills. After all, aren't risk-takers born, not made? Could Frankenberger have some sort of natural affinity for successful risk-taking? Some inherent ability to quickly, optimally calculate risk and then act in a way to ensure benefit? And is it possible that you'll find that predisposition written in his DNA?

AIN'T NOTHING BUT A GENE THING?

So what kind of genes might influence something as complex as risk-taking? One candidate of interest is the *DRD4* gene, which some call the "risk" gene. This little gene contains the blueprint for a specific type of dopamine receptor, the D4 receptor, which helps regulate how much dopamine flows through the mesocortical limbic circuit and, as we've learned, influences how we perceive risks.

How so, you might ask? Receptors play a critical role in synaptic transmission, or the propagation of brain signals across the cortex. When one brain cell releases a neurotransmitter, like dopamine, into the synapse, or the space between the cells, neighboring cells can then pick it up using specific receptors—unique proteins that reside on the cell's membrane. When there aren't as many D4 receptors in certain regulatory regions of the brain, dopamine may run rampant in the "gas" part of the circuitry, giving it quite a lot of influence over a risky decision. This appears to result in rewards being given more preference in a risk calculation than the potential negatives of going after them. The *DRD4* 7R+ allele, or gene variant, in particular, which denotes seven or more repeats of the variant, is a bit of code that has been linked to impulsive behaviors in individuals with attention-deficit/hyperactivity disorder as well as increased risk-taking in those without brain disorders.

Justin Garcia, an evolutionary biologist at Indiana University's Kinsey Institute, says that *DRD4* is very important from an evolutionary standpoint. The gene, and in particular the 7R+ variant, he notes, was likely selected for tens of thousands of years ago as humans started their great migrations out of Africa and into other parts of the world. The gene is implicated in impulsivity and novelty-seeking, two behaviors strongly related to risk-taking. Garcia argues that all that extra dopamine in the brain may have helped motivate prehistoric man to stop resting on his laurels and seek new territories for mates, food, and shelter. Those with the 7R+ variant were more likely to take risks. And so, they reaped the benefits.

Garcia, in partnership with J. Koji Lum, an anthropologist at Binghamton University—State University of New York, and a group of other interdisciplinary researchers were interested in how *DRD4* might translate into modern-day risk-taking behavior. The group recruited 98 males between the ages of 18 and 23 and measured whether they had the coveted 7R+ allele. A simple buccal wash with some mouthwash—swishing the liquid in your mouth and then spitting it into a test tube—gave the researchers all the DNA they needed to figure it out. And, as it just so happens, 24 of the participants had the variant of interest.

To determine the participants' penchant for risk-taking, the researchers had all 98 young men play a simple financial game. Each participant was given $250 to start. He could choose any portion of that original $250, from zero to the whole shebang, to gamble on a coin flip. If the participant won the coin flip, he'd take home 2.5 times the amount he'd invested in the gamble. If he lost, he'd lose the amount of the bet. So, if a participant decided to bet $100 of his original $250, he might win $250 on the coin flip, increasing his take-home cash to $500. If he lost the coin flip, however, he'd lose his $100 bet, taking home only $150. The study was set up so that there was potential to take home a good bit of cash if you were willing to take a risk and bet the majority of your stake.

When the researchers analyzed the data, they found that individuals with the 7R+ variant were much more likely to gamble in hopes of a bigger payout. This, they argue, suggests that this gene is linked to riskier decisions. Especially when you consider that this same group of researchers has shown similar effects with the 7R+ allele and sexual behavior—particularly, the overall number of sexual partners and the participation in riskier one-night stands—as well as how one bets in that nursing home card game favorite, bridge. Put it all together and it appears that the 7R+ variant has some definite sway over decision-making. Those with this variant tend to exhibit a lot more risky behaviors, across different tasks and environments.

"It's one gene and, of course, its contribution to a behavior as complex as risk-taking is going to be small. But those small differences can add up," Lum explains. "To a certain extent, assessing risk is just running an algorithm in your head. The different genetic variants mean that the algorithm is running at slightly different levels in different people. That's where all this comes together: People are running slightly different algorithms that help define whether or not they will take a risk. And, ultimately, over time, that one small difference in the algorithm ends up in very different lives lived."

Researchers at Northwestern University also found that *DRD4* variants influence financial risk-taking. And they discovered another gene of interest concerning risk: *5-HTTLPR,* a serotonin transporter gene. The D4 receptor isn't the only biological entity that can help dampen the dopamine. Serotonin, a fellow neurotransmitter, is often described as a dopamine brake: When it is released, dopamine loses some of its excitatory power. Translation: When there's lots of serotonin in the brain, rewards don't carry as much weight in the decision-making process as they do when there's a deluge of dopamine. The serotonin-transporting *5-HTTLPR* helps make sure there's plenty of serotonin around to balance out the dopamine. And it does so by moving serotonin out of the synapse and back into the original cell, so there's plenty around that can be used in future cell signaling.

At Northwestern, Camelia Kuhnen, a professor at the Kellogg School of Management, and Joan Chiao, a psychologist, examined these two genes as 65 study participants (26 men and 39 women) played a computer investment game. Over 96 trials, the individuals made decisions between risky and risk-free investments, without getting feedback on their overall performance during the course of the game. The participants also provided a bit of their DNA for genotyping. Kuhnen and Chiao found an interesting effect: Individuals with a particular shortened variant of *5-HTTLPR* were much more risk-averse, investing 28 percent less than those with a longer variant for that gene did. In contrast, having the 7R+ variant of *DRD4* resulted in a 25 percent increase in risky investments. Taken together, it would appear that having more serotonin in the brain decreases risk-taking, making it likely that individuals will put on the brakes. Having more dopamine, on the other hand, gives rewards more sway and increases risky behavior.

Additional studies have connected other dopamine-related genes to risk-taking too. A research group at the University of British Columbia found that skiers and snowboarders with a particular variant of the *DRD4* gene were more likely to take risks on the slopes—even after injury. Scientists have also linked other genes to changes in risk-taking behaviors. They found that catechol-O-methyltransferase, an enzyme that helps degrade dopamine and other neurotransmitters over time, seems to play a role in how we perceive and act on risk. Many other genes—probably including some still undiscovered—are involved with risky behavior.

Simply stated, there is not one "risk-taking" gene. Behaviors as complex as risk-taking have many, perhaps even hundreds, of individual genetic contributions. And each has the power to subtly, or perhaps not so subtly, influence the brain's natural decision-making algorithms.

"We assume that everyone is seeing and tasting and perceiving all the same things we are seeing and tasting and perceiving. But in reality, our brains all work differently—and that's because of all those little differences in our genes," says Lum. "So instead of assuming that everyone is equal and that this one gene is a little bit different for you and I, what we should be thinking is that we're all completely different. We could be playing the same hand of bridge, yet we're going to make different decisions on our bids because our brains find different levels of risk acceptable. We are just going to see the same information in a different way."

I don't need convincing—especially after watching Frankenberger play poker on some old ESPN Classic reruns. It's clear that he sees information in a different way than I do—and probably would at the poker table or the stock exchange. I'm not going to lie: I'm not even sure what an equity derivative is beyond what a quick Internet search tells me. I can't promise that I'd be very good at figuring out how to successfully trade them even with a lengthy, involved training program. And as for poker? When I do play, which isn't often, it's more for camaraderie than victory. But Frankenberger has managed to take on both Wall Street and the World Series of Poker with ease. When I ask him to explain his successes, to describe what he sees in a quick glance at the stock ticker or a hand of cards, he tells me that he focuses on the numbers.

"When you are working on Wall Street as a trader, everything you do is about risk management," Frankenberger says thoughtfully. "You're deciding how much risk you want to take, when to get in, and when to get out. You're maintaining your composure when things go against you. You try to separate the emotions involved with making or losing money from the ability to make the right decision. And those abilities translate to poker very well."

He explains, "Poker is the ultimate intellectual game. It has so many different challenges. You're not just running numbers in your head; you have to read the people you are playing. It's acting. It's perceiving other people. It's understanding how they perceive you. And it's math. And I'm a big math geek. I love thinking about numbers and working with numbers."

BUT WHAT ABOUT OPTIMIZING RISKS?

Different genetic variants, different brains, different acceptance levels—that makes sense. But, when looking at traits like risk-taking, it may seem as though we're talking about only your more negative behaviors. While bridge, gambling, promiscuous sex, arrests, and reckless driving might sound like fun in the abstract, those aren't the sorts of behaviors that necessarily lead to overall life success. Does genetics, by chance, tell us anything about helping individuals make more optimal decisions? About weighing risk appropriately against one's own self-interest? Maybe so, and it all has to do with an enzyme called monoamine oxidase A, which is responsible for breaking down powerful neurotransmitters like dopamine and rendering them inactive.

MAOA, the gene that makes monoamine oxidase A, is pretty darn interesting. It has been linked to a variety of neuropsychiatric conditions, including attention-deficit/hyperactivity disorder, anxiety disorders, autism, and antisocial personality disorder. It comes up time and time again when people look at the genetic contributions of impulsive behavior. A good number of incarcerated criminals have a variant of this gene that results in low expression too. And given that it creates an enzyme that breaks down neurotransmitters, it makes sense that it has such a reach. *MAOA* has also been implicated in aggressive behavior—and because of that particular association, as well as its links to crime, it has been nicknamed the "warrior" gene.

Cary Frydman, a neuroscientist at the California Institute of Technology, noted that sometimes, aggression and impulsivity aren't such bad things. After all, in some situations, being a little aggressive or a little impulsive might actually work in your favor. And that made him wonder if there was something a little different going on with the variants of this particular gene—if perhaps it wasn't as negative as some research had made it out to be.

To take a closer look, Frydman and his colleagues recruited 83 male volunteers, ages 19 to 27, to make some forced choices between gambles and sure things. Each study participant got 140 chances between taking a sure $2 or playing a 50-50 gamble to either gain $10 or lose $5. By setting the game up this way, the researchers could take a look at something beyond mere risk—they could see how the participants made decisions across the entire experiment. After all, the risk involved in one's choices may vary over the long term. An individual decision to gamble might look risky or impulsive, but, in some cases, it might actually offer the study participant a more beneficial option across the entire testing session. That benefit, of course, being the ability to go home with more money in your pocket. The researchers also took saliva from each participant to genotype for *MAOA,* the D4 receptor *DRD4,* and the serotonin transporter *5-HTTLPR.*

They found that individuals with *MAOA-L,* a variant of the so-called warrior gene, were better at comparing the risky option to the sure thing and then choosing the one that was most beneficial to them over the course of the entire experiment. These individuals ended up going home richer than those with other *MAOA* variants. Frydman suggests that these "warriors" aren't more impulsive or aggressive overall—rather, they are just very tuned into their own self-interest. What might look like impulsivity or aggression in other situations may simply be the *MAOA-L* carrier calculating and then responding with more focus to good opportunity. He argues that *MAOA-L* carriers are better at making optimal decisions, or decisions that will help them reach their intended goal, whether it be a bigger take-home payout after a neuroscience experiment or something more life-altering. After all, impulsive or aggressive behavior may be called for at times—it's not always a bad thing. It may be the way to get a fellow poker player to put more chips into the pot or to get the attention of a potential romantic interest. The context is important—and Frydman says that the *MAOA-L* variant may allow the carriers to really focus their attention, compare and contrast the potential risks and rewards, and then grab hold of better opportunities for success.

So, might Frankenberger have this warrior gene variant? Could be—though, as far as I know, no one has analyzed his saliva yet. I can say that he definitely enjoys his wins, and he repeatedly states that good decisions at the poker table involve careful analytical processing. "For me, the most important thing is using my analytical skills to figure out what's going on concerning betting patterns, timing, the size of the bets, and the cards you know," he says. "But you can also look at the other players. You can get a feel for how they look, for how they are playing. And that is going to be another factor, another in a series of inputs, that's going to inform my decisions at the table."

It's all very data-driven—and that kind of focus helps him play to win. And certainly, as I watch Frankenberger's past games, it's clear that he does occasionally play an aggressive hand in hopes of winning the game. It's just another part of his brand of risk management.

GENES AND RISK

....

To hear the genetics researchers tell it, successful risk-taking requires more than just running the numbers. There are important genetic components. I may not be as data-driven as Frankenberger, but, historically, I have been a risk-taker. It makes me wonder if you can see any evidence of that in my genes. Binghamton University's Lum is kind enough to run my *DRD4* genotype so that we can find out. I swish some mouthwash around my mouth for about 30 seconds, spit it into a test tube, and then mail the tube to Lum's lab. A few months later, he emails me with the results: I do not have the 7R+ variant.

"Your *DRD4* genotype is *4R/5R,*" he writes. "The 4 is the common, 'normal' allele, while the 5 is rare and has not been studied extensively. The assumption would be that your *4R/5R* genotype encodes the 'typical' response to sensation."

Basically, I don't have the risky form of the so-called risk gene. From a genetic standpoint, it seems that my mother's suspicion that I was born for trouble is unfounded—at least when it comes to one of my dopamine receptor genes. But, as Lum explains, it's just one gene. And the contribution of one gene to a behavior as complex and varied as risk-taking is always going to be fairly negligible. The answer to why people do the things they do—or why they perceive risks in the manner they do—is never going to be fully explained by genotyping. But, Lum argues, that one gene does add something to the baseline.

Different genes, different brains, different ways to assess and respond to risks. To anyone who has wondered why a sibling, partner, friend, or stranger has responded in a chancy way to a situation where you were compelled to play it safe, it makes some sense. And researchers have shown compelling links between risky behavior and specific variants of the *DRD4* and *MAOA* genes. But with tales of risk genes and warrior genes, it can be easy to take the genetic story a little too far. Christopher Chabris, a psychologist at

Union College who studies the genetic contributions to complex traits, says that, as sample sizes have gotten larger and our genotyping techniques more sophisticated, we're learning that many genes we thought were associated with things like intelligence, empathy, or risk-taking are actually false positives. In other words, as geneticists expand their studies, those very genes we've nicknamed "risk" or "warrior" may not play as strong a role in those behaviors after all.

"The most important thing to understand about genetic studies of any complex trait is that individual genetic variants will have only very small effects," Chabris says. "The general lesson we've learned as we've done more of these kinds of studies is that human behavioral traits are influenced by hundreds, perhaps even thousands, of common genetic variants. And that's the real challenge. If the effects are tiny—if, say, each variant has only a very minuscule effect—it's hard to find something outside of noise unless you have a really, really large sample size. Like a sample size in the order of tens or hundreds of thousands."

None of the genetic studies regarding risk-taking, thus far, has even come close to those kind of numbers. Which raises the question: Will the studies that have implicated *DRD4* or *MAOA* in risk-taking hold up over time? The jury is still out. And as researchers conduct further genetic studies on risk-taking behavior, new genes of interest will be discovered. But here's the thing: We need to think beyond single genes. As Chabris says, any behavioral trait is going to be influenced by hundreds, if not thousands, of common genetic variants. So, there's no point in getting too hung up on *DRD4* or *MAOA*. What's more important is that scientists are showing that a variety of our genes do have a say in just how we perceive risks—and that's the message we should be taking to heart.

I must make one more important caveat here: Any genetic contribution to risk-taking is probabilistic rather than deterministic. What does that mean? Just because you happen to carry the risk gene, or any particular variant of any correlated gene, doesn't mean you are necessarily going to be someone who is always engaging in risky behavior. Just because you don't have one of these genotypes doesn't mean you won't. Look at me: I don't have the 7R+ allele, but I feel like I've been a risk-taker for most of my life.

Any behavior is the result of a complex interaction of both biology and environment. And while people with a certain genetic makeup may have a strong biological predisposition to engage in some risky business—to see opportunity where most of us would see danger—they still have their frontal lobes, the "brakes," if you will, to help them temper their desires with a little old-fashioned reason.

I'm living proof of that. Despite any past proclivities for risk-taking, I've been riding my brakes pretty hard lately. Too hard, if you ask me. If I do have other genes beyond *DRD4* that predispose me to risky business, I'm managing to keep them in check without too much difficulty. So, you see, genetics studies are important because they give us an idea of how differently people's brains may be wired when it comes to risk and decision-making— how they may relay neurochemical signals differently when faced with a risky situation. But, as Lum argues, no matter how attracted you may be to a risk, there is always a "cognitive override" option.

Our prefrontal cortices, our slow-thinking brake systems, mean you can always choose to play it safe.

"We all have urges. Very few of us get to do everything we want to do. So everyone has brakes that they put on their desires as they move through life. Some people just have the kind of biology that requires them to put on more brakes than others," Lum says with a smile.

I do not know what may lurk in Andy Frankenberger's genetic profile. I have no idea if he possesses one of these risk-taking variants—or if he requires more effort to put on the brakes than others. But, to be honest, even if I did know, while it would give me a few interesting insights into his behaviors (and perhaps his successes), it wouldn't tell me all I need to know.

Why might that be? Because no one gene is dictating our response to risk. Rather, our different genetic variants mean that my perceived reality and yours may be quite different. Similarly, my response to a particular situation, and the risks involved, may be different from yours too.

Frankenberger understands that implicitly—and even uses that information, though he may not even be aware of it, at the poker table. He reads his fellow players, as well as the cards. He observes how they respond to different situations and then uses that information to help inform his next play. No genetic tests required.

"At the core, what makes someone a good poker player is being a good decision-maker," Frankenberger tells me. "It's about being able to cut to the core of a problem and break down complex situations into the most basic things—and focus on the things you should be focused on while you make those decisions. But I suppose those are the kind of skills that help you when you're making any big decisions in life."

Chapter Five

....

RISK AND GENDER

LET'S PLAY A GAME. Sit back, relax, and conjure up the person who, for you, personifies successful risk-taking. Imagine that person in full Technicolor glory—perhaps in the midst of taking that famous risk you admire so much.

I don't know who you selected. But I'm guessing you picked a person with a lot of gumption. A person who is achievement-oriented, focused on the goal against seemingly insurmountable odds. This risk-taker is confident and strong—and stands just on the sane side of the crazy line. This is someone who inspires a great deal of admiration (and even a little bit of confusion) when you look at the accomplishments—and the path to them. This person is a doer, not a spectator. Someone who somehow manages to do the things that the rest of us believe just can't be done.

And, likely, the person you're thinking of has some balls. And I'm speaking literally here.

That's right. I'm guessing that the vast majority of you, when you conjured up your risk-taker, thought of a man. Maybe a male race car driver, professional athlete, soldier, or cop. It's not all that surprising. We tend to assume males are naturally more risk-taking than females. And it goes beyond simple sexism; it's an idea fully backed, historically, by science. Whether or not we take risks has quite a bit to do with what we have between our legs—and the corresponding hormones that run rampant in our bodies and brains.

Captain L. Davis, a veteran firefighter with the Skyland Fire Rescue near Asheville, North Carolina, is someone who quickly pops into my mind when I think of a successful risk-taker. Firefighting is a dangerous gig, with a high potential for injury and death. And, like most firefighters, Davis is a bit of the hero type. This captain is strong, capable, and courageous. Not to mention unafraid of running into burning buildings. Davis is also quite modest, in an "Aw, shucks" kind of way. So when I ask what motivates firefighters to run smack into danger while so many others are naturally inclined to shy away from it, I'm expecting to hear some canned line about how "someone's got to do it," or perhaps something about how everything just falls away when it's time to help someone in distress. Instead, Davis tells me that many firefighters love the job because of the "rush," the thrill of dealing with a volatile situation.

"A lot of them say there's really nothing that compares to it," Davis tells me in a gruff and rather detached manner. As if "rush" as a career-motivating force is a given.

"And you? Do you like the rush of it?" I ask, somewhat incredulously, trying to imagine any circumstance that might inspire me to willingly approach and enter a burning building. Outside of saving the life of my child (and as much as I love my kid, I can even see myself hesitating if there were a trained professional nearby), I can think of nary a one.

"Yeah, absolutely. We don't actually catch fires all that often. We spend most of our time doing training or EMS [emergency medical service] calls," Davis says emphatically. "But when we actually catch a fire, there's nothing like rushing into a burning building. It's a lot of fun."

Talk about balls. And, as you might imagine, the fire department where Davis works could fairly be called a bit of a boys' club. Fire-fighting, as a profession overall, generally is. The work is physically, mentally, and emotionally rigorous—and there are many who just don't have what it takes to get the job done. So when I ask Davis about the prevalence of women in local firefighting circles, I'm not surprised at the answer.

"There are a few women. There are some drivers and one newly promoted lieutenant that I know of for sure," Davis says. "I don't have a total headcount, but, if I had to guess, I'd say there are probably about 15 female firefighters across the city. And that's out of about 300 department employees."

Only 15 out of 300—that's a pretty small percentage. When you look at similar high-risk professions like serving in the armed forces or a police department, the male-to-female ratios are pretty similar. And those statistics fall in line with the stereotypes we hold about risk-taking and gender. You know, the whole "boys will be boys" attitude in response to loud, rough-and-tumble, and risky behaviors. And, on the other side of the coin, the idea that girls are, by nature, "better angels," quieter and more timid than your average male.

It may sound like an outdated stereotype straight out of a 1950s sitcom. But, historically, scientific studies have suggested that the stereotype exists for a reason. Why, might you ask? Well, for starters, out of all the biological predictors for behavioral risk-taking, one of the most prognostic is simply being the owner of a Y chromosome—in short, being male. Statistically, men are more likely than women to get in fights, drive aggressively, participate in extreme sports, develop alcohol problems, gamble, and get arrested. Not that women are completely immune to those particular extra-curricular activities, mind you. But, overall, females just don't represent the same way when it comes to dangerous behaviors. In fact, study after study shows that, all things being equal, men are simply more likely to live dangerously than women.

There's an evolutionary argument to be made for why this is so. You've probably heard the story that men are more risk-taking than women because of their responsibilities. Males need to go out and hunt to provide for their families; females need to stay home and tend to the offspring. But there's a little more to it than that. In the animal kingdom, the larger of the sexes in any species—and, in the case of humans, that would be the male—is genetically programmed to branch out and find new territory. Doing so helps reproductively viable animals find mates, as well as new sources of food and shelter. Plus, of course, avoid those disagreeable incestuous entanglements that may result in less-than-stellar offspring down the line. Having a little biological edge in the area of risk-taking helps the males go out and explore, helping to ensure that the species will survive (and, with luck, thrive) in the future. Makes sense, I suppose. But I can't help thinking that females, too, would benefit from some of those risk-related perks. So why should boys have all the fun?

THE GAS OF TESTOSTERONE

....

History and stereotypes might make you think there is some kind of biological attribute that has given men a risk-taking edge—some hormone or neurochemical, an integral part of "maleness," that makes them more inclined to go for the risky decision. Scientists have considered that too. The first thing that came to mind was testosterone, the primary sex hormone in males.

Researchers at Harvard University wondered if testosterone might offer some answers to the sex differences observed. And lo and behold, when they took a look at testosterone in stock market traders, they found something rather interesting. Folks on the stock market floor showed their greatest profits on days when their testosterone was up. You see, testosterone levels fluctuate. Have some sex, flirt with a pretty girl, or participate in some intense exercise, and testosterone rises. And, here, the researchers found there was also a correlation between heightened testosterone and higher profits.

While the finding was provocative, it offered a bit of a chicken-and-egg-problem. Were higher levels of testosterone helping the traders take more (and perhaps smarter) risks? Or was testosterone raised in response to a successful day? No one knew.

Here's what scientists did know. High testosterone levels aren't just linked to success on the trading floor. Men with high levels of testosterone are a bit of a type—and tend to push the envelope. You'll know a high-testosterone male when you see him. He's healthy, virile, and strong. He tends to be a risk-taker, breaking rules and flouting authority at every turn. He may, like Davis, be into situations that provide some "rush." He is charming, outgoing, and, yes, even egocentric. And he's someone who would totally go for a hero-type job; there are probably more than a few of these macho dudes in Davis's fire department.

So, might elevated testosterone predict riskier behaviors? To help tease out the answer, Coren Apicella, an anthropologist at Harvard, and an interdisciplinary team of researchers decided to look at how testosterone influenced men playing a simple financial game. Apicella is the researcher who initially recruited the cohort of young men for a cheek-swab study about gambling—the study that generated the data Justin Garcia and J. Koji Lum used to observe how the *DRD4* gene affects risk-taking behavior. A total of ninety-eight males between the ages of 18 and 23 participated in the study. Each participant provided a testosterone level just before playing the game: A simple saliva sample provided a baseline measure of the sex hormone. Each participant was also assessed for facial masculinity as well as the 2D:4D ratio, the difference of length between the second and fourth fingers of each hand.

If you are wondering why the scientists took facial assessments and digit lengths when they had a direct testosterone measure from the saliva, it's because doing so allowed them to get a glimpse of an individual's testosterone history. The same high testosterone levels correlated with all those macho behaviors listed above are also linked with the development of a chiseled, masculine face during puberty. Think Hugh Jackman or Javier Bardem—you know, that tough and manly face with a strong brow ridge and rather robust jawline. The facial assessment offers some data about how much testosterone a study participant might have been working with during the adolescent years.

And the finger lengths? Well, a high testosterone level in the womb slows the growth of the index finger relative to the other digits, resulting in a smaller difference between the length of the index finger and the ring finger. So, the shape of a man's face and the length of his digits offer us clues about not only his current testosterone level but also his testosterone levels at different points in his development. Taken together, these measurements offer an overall testosterone profile for a guy over his life span.

After collecting all this testosterone-related information, Apicella and colleagues had the study participants make a decision on a gamble. Just to repeat, this was the task: Each participant was given $250 to start: He could choose any portion of that original $250, from zero to the entire amount, to gamble on a coin flip. If the participant won the coin flip, he'd take home 2.5 times the amount he'd invested in the gamble. If he lost, he'd lose the amount of his bet. The study was set up so that there was the potential to take home more than $600 if you were willing to bet big.

It may not surprise you to learn that Apicella's team found that men with higher levels of testosterone at baseline, or before they gambled, were more likely to risk more money. While Apicella would be quick to tell you that this association cannot pinpoint causality—that is, the data can't tell you that all that extra testosterone is definitely *causing* those men to make riskier bets—she does think that testosterone plays an important role in risk-taking behavior. And, incidentally, other studies show that these testosterone-risk effects are present in all risk-takers, not just the male ones.

That's right: The bodies of ladies, too, produce the stuff of which masculine men are made. Testosterone, despite always being referred to as a "male" hormone, can also be found *en force* in women, just as estrogen, the "female" hormone, is present in males. In fact, estrogen and testosterone are eerily similar molecules. Each can work with the other's receptors in the body and brain—and, if you add the enzyme aromatase, which we all have a lot of in our bodies, it will actually transform testosterone into estrogen. It makes you wonder why we insist on having these gender-specific connotations regarding these hormones in the first place—especially when you consider that researchers have linked high testosterone levels to risky behaviors in women too.

Paola Sapienza, a professor at Northwestern University's Kellogg School of Management, wondered why women seemed to be more risk-averse in economics—something she had seen firsthand at the school itself. She noted that only a small percentage of female MBA students from Kellogg, a top-tier business school, went on to higher risk (and higher profit) financial careers after graduation. And it was something that irked her. Why were so many smart, capable women purposely avoiding these kind of go-getter gigs? She wondered whether testosterone was involved—and decided to take an empirical look to investigate.

Sapienza and colleagues recruited nearly 500 MBA students from the University of Chicago Booth School of Business to play a financial risk game—and give up a little hormonal data—to see whether there was an interaction between testosterone and risk. As in Apicella's study, testosterone levels were assessed using finger-length ratios as well as by saliva sample. Then, participants played a computer game to measure risky behavior.

Over 15 trials, participants were asked to choose between a guaranteed but varying dollar amount (between \$50 and \$120) and a riskier lottery that would pay either a higher amount (\$200) or zero dollars with equal probability. So, in one trial, you could choose between a guaranteed \$75, say, or playing the lottery for \$200 or nothing. The idea is that the more risk-averse folks will always choose the fixed dollar amount—but risk-takers, on the other hand, will go for the gamble in hopes of winning more.

The study yielded results that fit right in with Apicella's work. Men, overall, opted to play the lottery more often than did women—significantly more so. But a fair number of the women opted to gamble too. And the woman who did so had significantly higher levels of testosterone than those who chose to play it safe. Once again, higher testosterone levels were significantly correlated with riskier behaviors—in both men and women.

The effect wasn't limited to the game either; testosterone was associated with real-world decisions too. The researchers decided to follow the participants after graduation and look at what kind of positions they took after receiving their degrees. And, interestingly enough, they found that testosterone levels were linked to what kind of jobs the female students accepted after graduation. The higher the testosterone level, the riskier the type of job the woman took in the finance sector. In this case, a higher testosterone level was predictive.

Taken together, it's clear that higher levels of testosterone are linked to riskier behaviors. And since men naturally have more of this sex hormone, one might argue that boys have a bit of a biological push when it comes to risk. But that does not mean women are completely risk-averse. On the contrary, testosterone is also linked to riskier behaviors in women—both in simple gambling tasks and more real-world applications like what kind of career you go into after graduation. It would appear that when it comes to risk, testosterone is straddling the gender divide.

THE "BETTER ANGELS" OF RISK-TAKING

Of course, financial tasks encapsulate only one type of risk. Perhaps we'd see more scientific evidence supporting men as natural-born risk-takers if we broadened our definition somewhat. After all, when you think of a risk-taker, you are probably more likely to envision an extreme snowboarder or a skydiver than a chief financial officer. And, certainly, past research in psychology has suggested that men are more prone to getting their thrill on by participating in what are called sensation-seeking behaviors.

A sensation-seeker is a specific type of risk-taker. He (or she) is the kind of person who is always on the lookout for new, intense, and varied experiences. Sensation-seekers throw themselves into the unknown, often just for the high of it—and have no qualms about facing physical, social, legal, and financial risks in order to do so. Marvin Zuckerman, the psychologist who first described sensation-seeking, believes there are four specific components of the behavior: thrill-seeking, experience-seeking, disinhibition, and boredom susceptibility. High-sensation seekers tend to appreciate activities that result in a "rush," like skydiving or flying (or, in Davis's case, handling a fire); seek out new and unfamiliar experiences through travel, drug use, or unconventional relationships; want the feeling of being out of control; and, finally, are unable to handle boredom. Unsurprisingly, high-sensation seekers find situations in which they aren't being adequately stimulated to be all but intolerable—and tend to take more risks than your average bear.

Historically, sensation-seekers were considered to be predominantly male. But a recent meta-analysis, conducted by researchers at the University of St. Andrews in Scotland, found something interesting when they looked at differences in sensation-seeking across dozens of studies. The group found that, overall, when it comes to qualities like disinhibition and boredom susceptibility, men still reign supreme. Women, it seems, are less offended by monotony and show more of a preference for being in control than the boys do. That's as true today as it was 50 years ago, when Zuckerman first started his sensation-seeking research.

But, when it comes to thrill- and adventure-seeking behaviors, the gender divide is not quite so divided. Today, scientists don't see as much of a gap between males and females in these kinds of risk-taking arenas. And we aren't seeing it outside the laboratory either. Twenty years ago, the vast majority of sponsored extreme sports athletes were men. Today, the North Face, a high-performance outdoor sporting equipment company, sponsors 17 women on its roster of 56 athletes. No, it's not a 50-50 split. But 30 percent ain't bad.

The research suggests that sensation-seeking in women has changed simply because times have changed. Social norms now allow women to pursue adventure. And the real world appears to support that notion. We ladies aren't expected to sit in our living rooms, ankles crossed, while completing complicated cross-stitch patterns anymore. We are able, and even encouraged, to do all manner of fun and risky outdoor activities these days.

Another factor is at play too. And that's increased comfort in admitting a love for thrill and adventure. Most of us have stories about some distant female relative who marched for suffrage against her husband's wishes, emigrated to the United States with nothing but a silk shawl and a few coins to her name, or perhaps had a few wild love affairs during a time when most women were married off by age 18—and I'm only talking about my family here. But as much as we might like to discuss those crazy old broads, it's doubtful that their immediate families would have been as happy to reveal their shenanigans in the moment. They were flouting social niceties, after all. As society has grown more accepting of women getting out in the world in search of independence and adventure, we no longer think about some of our more wild behaviors with shame. We are happy to make the skeletons in our closets dance and tell you all about it. After all, if it's now more socially acceptable for women to travel solo to Africa or to heli-ski, they are going to be much more willing to admit to those adventures when queried about them in a risk-taking study.

So, what we see today is that women are taking their fair share of risks. More than a few were probably doing so before. But "socially transmitted information," that information that disperses cultural values and social norms while perpetuating the status quo, can influence behavior (and the reporting of such behavior) when it comes to risk.

The importance of socially transmitted information starts to stick with you when you more closely consider risk-taking studies and the kind of tasks scientists use to measure risk. Most focus on financial-type tasks and money lotteries. That's a pretty niche category. Would males continue to seem like the predominantly risky sex if we looked at the sex differences involved in other types of risky behavior? Maybe not.

Bernd Figner, a researcher investigating risky decision-making at Radboud University Nijmegen in the Netherlands, and his colleague Elke Weber were curious about what may be behind the sex differences that so many researchers observed in risk-taking studies. In a review that looked at a variety of risk-taking measures, Figner and Weber found that, in fact, females take plenty of risks—they just don't tend to go all in when it comes to commonly used monetary gambles. Where you'll see women showing a good bit of risky behavior is in the social arena, which may be a place they feel more comfortable taking on uncertainty. Studies indicate that women are much more likely to bring up an unpopular issue with a group or even change careers later in life than men are—things that are fairly risky when you thoroughly consider them.

"The evidence that women are always going to be more risk-averse than men is not so clear-cut and simple as many have made it out to be," Figner says. "One important factor that helps to explain why someone takes a risk and someone does not is familiarity with the situation. As you become more familiar with a situation, your perception of the risks changes."

Figner suggests that the reason why men tend to go for the gamble in these kinds of experiments is that they are simply more familiar with financial tasks. "Historically, women just didn't have much experience with risky financial decisions. We think that explains the lower risk tendency that so many researchers have shown in that domain. But it's different in other life domains. And research has shown that females are actually greater risk-takers than males when it comes to more social decisions."

Margareta Bohlin, a researcher who studies adolescent risk-taking at University West in Sweden, has observed similar trends in her own work. Her ongoing research in risk-taking behaviors suggests that the sex differences are often a by-product of what is considered culturally acceptable for men and women. Think about it: It wasn't that long ago that extreme sports and many other risky activities were frowned upon for women—meaning that women might not have had the opportunity to partake even if they had an interest in such things. If they did partake, they might not be inclined to share that information for fear of ridicule or condemnation. Today, however, women can do it all. Scuba diving, exotic travel, and mountain climbing are activities that both men and women commonly participate in. We are even encouraged to pursue degrees in engineering and computer science! But all that artifact about what's socially acceptable, what women and men should and shouldn't do, still has the power to color the way we perceive risks.

"What is seen as a risk, and defined as such, changes over time. Something we would not consider a risk may have been seen as very risky a couple of decades ago. And vice versa. Think about smoking. A few decades ago, it was not considered a risky behavior. Now we know it is very dangerous," Bohlin says. "My studies show that, although women perceive risks to be more dangerous than men do, they end up participating in risky activities to the same degree that men do. Women are now more free to take part in activities that, earlier, would have been regarded as activities for men only."

More and more studies are showing the same trend. Girls are representing on risky, sensation-seeking activities that were once considered culturally verboten. And they are more than keeping up with the boys as they do so. But Bohlin has found one interesting difference.

In a series of interviews and group discussions that assessed risk-taking, Bohlin discovered that women tended to evaluate different situations as being riskier than males did. Yet they still reported partaking in extreme sports, partying, and uncommitted sex, despite having more concerns about the risks involved. Consistently, Bohlin saw a difference in perception but not in actual behavior—in risk and sensation-seeking. Why might that be?

"It may not sound logical, but attitudes are often more difficult to change than behavior," Bohlin says. "Values and norms are firm and pretty resistant to change. So we tend to change our behaviors earlier than the attitudes surrounding them."

I can't help thinking again of Davis's firefighting department, with about 15 women in a cadre of 300 firefighters. It's a striking (and slightly disappointing) ratio. And yet, I'd hazard a guess that, 20 or 30 years ago, there wasn't a single female on the Skyland firefighting team. In my grandmother's day, the idea of a woman firefighter would have been considered downright dangerous, both for that woman and for the people she was supposed to be protecting. I imagine more than a few people would make the same argument about women on the force today. So, while 15 active female firefighters might not seem like all that many, the fact that there are any on the force at all supports the idea that, while attitudes may be slow to change, behaviors certainly are doing so.

THE BOTTOM LINE

We've long assumed that men have the risk-taking market covered. That all their testosterone confers a distinct biological advantage when it comes to hitting the gas. But despite the wealth of history denoting males as risk-taking go-getters and females as risk-averse types, the truth isn't quite that simple.

Take Davis, as an example. As we discussed Davis's work and love of the firefighting "rush," I may have forgotten to mention something kind of important. The "L"? It stands for Leah. That's right, this direct and gruff veteran firefighter is a 44-year-old mother of two. Her strength and tenacity—not to mention her choice of occupation—challenge the idea that risk-taking is only for the boys.

"Firefighting is a very physical job. It's not feminine in the least. You get absolutely filthy when you work. It's not glamorous, that's for sure," she says, laughing. "As a woman, I certainly wouldn't say I fit into the normal, not around [the firehouse] anyway. But I love what I do. And it's a good fit for me."

That it is. Davis brings into practical view exactly what today's studies show experimentally: that sex differences in risk-taking are not as vast as once thought. And, as society becomes more accepting of women taking risks, the gap is closing. Davis, despite her two X chromosomes, has always been fascinated by firefighting—it was a childhood dream of hers to work in the field.

"It's always intrigued me. I started out volunteering for the department. At the time, I was in school and had other career plans. I was like six months away from moving away to pursue vet school but then, on a whim, applied for a permanent job with the fire department," she tells me. "I got it and was like, 'I have to do this.' "

Vet school might have been the more socially appropriate choice for a woman at that time—but Davis wanted something different. And having found her true vocation, she's never looked back.

As a captain, Davis now evaluates new recruits in the department. When I ask her what makes a successful firefighter, she is quick to answer. "Honestly, you need to have something in your nature to do this job well. You need to be flexible and adaptable because things can change in a second. You need to be disciplined, particularly when starting out, and just get on the truck and do what you're told and be OK with that. You have to be able to work as a team, speak up if you feel unsafe, and continuously train and get better," she says. "It's not easy."

Notice that she doesn't mention gender in that list of qualities. She's living proof that it doesn't matter.

That's the thing: It would be all too easy to just say men have a biological predisposition to risk and leave it at that. But there are all sorts of different kinds of risks in the world—and as society changes, as our values change, and as our ideas about gender change, our ideas about risk change too. They have to. Today, women are taking their fair share of risks—and finding success in the boardroom, the hospital, the trading floor, the research lab, the stadium, and other arenas that were previously closed to them. As Margareta Bohlin says, attitudes can be a tough thing to change. But we need to start shifting our more outdated notions concerning risk and gender if we are to have any chance of truly understanding how people approach risk in the real world.

So, the next time someone asks you to imagine a risk-taker, let your mind go a little broader. And, yes, that bad pun was intentional. I bet, if you give it a second or two, you can actually think of quite a few female risk-takers—women who inspire (and perhaps confuse) you with their gumption, strength, and determination. Women who manage all manner of incredible feats that the rest of us are told just can't be done. Women who support what scientists keep learning: that risky behavior is part and parcel of living, no matter what you've got going on downstairs.

Chapter Six

....

RISK AND AGE

IF YOU CAME OF AGE IN THE 1980s, as I did, you are likely familiar with the movie *Lethal Weapon*. Two mismatched police detectives unexpectedly find themselves partnered up: Martin Riggs, the loose cannon with revenge on his mind, and Roger Murtaugh, the older, wiser man of the force, just counting the days until retirement. When I saw this film for the first time in high school, I identified with the loonier of the two, Riggs. He might be a little crazy but, man, he was fun. Also, easy on the eyes. When I watched the film recently, however, I discovered that my sympathies had changed. Today, you'll find me more in Murtaugh's corner. Mostly because I find myself, as a middle-aged mom, inadvertently quoting his signature line from the film, "I'm too old for this shit," on a regular basis.

As I said, I used to be a risk-taker. But now, when I consider new adventures, I tend to take the Murtaugh point of view. I just feel too old to bother. The potential negative consequences of a risky decision, like the loss of financial or social stability, seem just too great to bear. I have a mortgage to pay, for goodness' sake! I have a kid to raise (and to drive to tae kwon do class on time). And the positive outcomes? Well, they just don't seem quite as compelling as they once did. But as I find myself settling way too easily into my comfort zone, I can't help wondering why my approach has changed so much. Am I really too old for this shit? Has my age and place in society somehow affected the way I'm perceiving and pursuing risk? What's changed in me since my crazy, risk-taking teenage years?

THE TEEN SPECIES

Jonathan is not the kid you think of when someone mentions your typical risk-taking teenager. At 18, he is an above-average student, secretary of the student council, and a star player on his school's soccer team. He is friendly and well liked across his school's diverse social strata. When his peers call him one of the most popular boys in the senior class, they don't say it with any undercurrent of derision—they add it to his biography as a sign of respect. He has already been accepted to his college of choice, with a sports scholarship to help defray the not insignificant cost of his tuition. His teachers often point to him as a school success story, someone who seems to effortlessly balance the stresses of school and sports. He surrounds himself with other hardworking, well-rounded students—good kids who make up the school band, the science club, and the sports teams. Everyone in his life expects him to do great things. And he seems fairly unaffected by the weight of those expectations. He's the kind of kid who makes the teen years look good.

But even for Jonathan, adolescence is not an easy process. It is painful for the teens and for everyone who interacts with them. It's a volatile time, both physically and emotionally. Abigail Baird, a brain researcher at Vassar College, says that what you see on the outside is happening in the teenage brain as well.

"You see that explosive growth and the gawkiness that comes with it on the outside during adolescence—kids suddenly shooting up with long, clumsy arms and legs. What shouldn't be surprising, then, is that there's that same gawkiness when we're talking about the brain too. It's not an exaggeration to say that things are exploding in terms of brain growth," she says. "Everything is changing, and it's changing really, really fast."

And it's those changes, neuroscientists argue, that make teenagers the ultimate risk-takers.

"The biggest source of morbidity and mortality in young people, not only in the United States but in industrialized countries, in general, is not medical disease but problems with behavior and emotion," says Ronald Dahl, a researcher at the University of California, Berkeley's School of Public Health. "We're talking about suicide, homicide, car accidents, substance abuse, and sexual risk-taking. There is something about the neurobiology of adolescents that makes them more likely to take risks than children or adults. We're only beginning to understand it."

That includes the so-called good kids like Jonathan. Dahl explains, "Eighty percent of adolescents don't do wild and crazy things. But even the shy, anxious kids tend to become more exploratory and more likely to experiment during mid- to late adolescence."

Jonathan may have a good head on his shoulders but, after a thorough talk, I soon learn that he also has an unapologetic penchant for partying. He and his friends spend their weekends, when they aren't on the soccer pitch, hopping from friend's house to friend's house, drinking alcohol acquired by older siblings and the odd well-made fake ID. They drink too much, drive too fast, and "hook up" with girls at every available opportunity.

"There's a lot of partying around here," Jonathan says, shrugging. "Our parents are pretty busy with their own stuff, and there's not much else to do. So we hang out and find ways to blow off steam."

As Jonathan and his friends tell me about some of their most recent exploits, I soon learn that ways to "blow off steam" include random (and sometimes unprotected) sex, drug use, fistfights, skipping school and home responsibilities, driving under the influence, and jumping off a second-story roof into a neighboring home's swimming pool. All pursuits that, even when taking into account the natural teenage gift for exaggeration, may have the power to dramatically alter the path of a perfect high school golden boy.

A BRAIN DISCONNECT

Jonathan will be the first to tell you that he knows better. "I mean, I don't want to say any of that stuff is a good idea—it's not. But it's fun," he says. "Sometimes I think I should have just stayed home and worked on [soccer] drills or studied or something instead of going to the party. And if I have practice the next day, I think, 'Oh, I should not have drank that much.' But I never think any of that [while I'm partying]."

As many of us remember from our own adolescence, when it comes to risky business, it's not that teens don't know any better. They know that underage drinking may lead to physical illness, trouble with their parents, or removal from a coveted place on the school soccer team. They are well aware that unprotected sex has the potential to make them parents or give them sexually transmitted diseases at a vulnerable age. Adolescents can easily parrot any bit of that information back to us with remarkable sincerity. For example, when I ask Jonathan, "Is it a good idea or bad idea to have unprotected sex?" he is very quick to reply.

"It's a horrible idea. You should always protect yourself." But when I push, and ask why he has participated in unprotected sex before, he pauses to think before responding. "It's a horrible idea. I know it's a horrible idea. Unless you're right there and you don't have protection, maybe. But still it's a horrible idea."

"Aren't you worried about getting a girl pregnant?"

He gives me a noncommittal shrug. "Like I said, unprotected sex is a horrible idea. I know that."

He doesn't try to justify his behavior. He has sat through enough sex education classes to know that he can't. But knowledge isn't always the most important factor when you find yourself making a decision in the moment. So, despite the known consequences, teens still often act unwisely. There seems to be some kind of disconnect between knowing and doing in the teenage brain—and new work in neuroscience suggests that this disconnect is literal as well as figurative.

Laurence Steinberg, a social neuroscientist at Temple University, has proposed that teens are more likely to indulge in risky business because of the way their brains are maturing. Right around puberty, when sex hormones are working their magic on our reproductive systems, they are also heralding some pretty dramatic changes in our brains. These alterations result in significant differences in how the brain processes dopamine—which not only affects the brain's risk-and-reward processing circuitry but also mediates social and emotional behaviors.

At around the age of ten, urged on by sex steroids and other important growth hormones, the brain starts to prune dopamine receptors in the striatum, an important part of the basal ganglia, and the prefrontal cortex. This pruning changes the relative density of receptors in the circuit linking the area of the brain involved with processing rewards (the basal ganglia) and the area of the brain implicated in inhibition and control (the prefrontal cortex). The changes in receptors mean that dopamine is flowing somewhat unencumbered. And the result is a mesocortical limbic system that is a bit out of sync, with amped up emotion and motivation coupled with dampened inhibition and long-term planning capability. Basically, you see an increase in gas and a decrease in brakes—or, the perfect neural recipe for a sensation-seeking wild child. Looking back at my own teen years, which were fraught with more than a bit of crazy, it certainly makes perfect sense to me.

These dramatic changes to the brain have led Vassar's Baird to suggest adolescence is much like a second toddlerhood. When she first tells me this, I laugh. But on further reflection, I can see her point. The toddler years are a sensitive period of growth in both the body and brain that helps babies transition into kids. And when I look closer at the behavior of Jonathan and his friends (not to mention the adolescent exploits of myself and my own friends), I see more overlap than I care to admit. "That's not fair" type tantrums? Check. Pushing boundaries? Of course. A proclivity for hyperbole? Sure. Sensation-seeking? Yep. A "me, me, me" mentality? Oh, yeah. Baird argues that while these particular qualities are not always the most fun for parents or teachers, they underlie the adolescent brain's amazing capacity to learn and grow.

"Think about it. If you want to learn that second language or learn the skills to become that superstar jock, adolescence is the time to do it," says Baird. "Everything is just exploding neurally, and there is an unprecedented amount of learning that takes place. Just like toddlers are making that leap, learning all they need to go from babyhood to childhood, teens need to get out there and find ways to learn the skills they need to become adults."

Studies out of Baird's lab and others suggest that those out-of-control emotions and bewildering motivations that so many parents wish they could quash are actually important to all that critical pre-adult learning. "The teen years require a lot of trial and error," Baird says. "If everything wasn't so dramatic and important and emotional, adolescents wouldn't have the motivation they need to get back up and do it again when they fail. And if they are going to gain the experience they need to learn how to make good decisions, they have to get back up and do it again. And again. And again."

And doing something again and again and again is going to provide the necessary experience so that teens can, over time, sync those important brain gas and brake systems. Which will get the mesocortical limbic circuit working to its best ability so that teens can become the (mostly) responsible and dependable adults we know that they one day can be.

PROCESSING RISK AND REWARDS

So why is everything so dramatic and important and emotional? It comes back to the neurotransmitter dopamine. A toned-down frontal lobe paired with an intensified emotion and motivation circuit is the perfect recipe for risk-taking. But while Berkeley's Ronald Dahl says it's easy to suggest that hormones make teens temporarily crazy or unable to use their frontal cortices appropriately, those notions are incorrect. Jonathan, for the most part, is the kind of kid who thinks things through. For example, he has asked me to use a pseudonym for this chapter—although, to be fair, he's avoiding the risk of annoying his family more than the risk of damaging any future career plans. Yet, despite that rationality, his teenage brain strengthens the power of rewards so that he will be motivated to gain the experience required to grown and learn. And one way it is doing so is in how rewards are perceived.

Recent work by B. J. Casey and her colleagues at Cornell University suggests that the teen brain processes risks the same way that adult brains do, with one important difference: Areas of the brain involved with reward processing, like the ventral striatum, part of the basal ganglia, are much more active, as measured by increased cerebral blood flow, in teens than in younger children or adults. The implication is that this increased activity results in teens overestimating the value of rewards. When we consider Jonathan's decision to skip using a condom, his brain magnified the reward involved with a hookup. His brain, with its out-of-sync setup, was telling him that he couldn't pass up this encounter: This sex will be the sexiest sex of all time. It became a reward fantastic enough to outdo all other considerations, including the potential consequences of teenage pregnancy or venereal disease.

Baird says that the exaggerated value of rewards serves a purpose. "Really wanting those rewards is to our advantage when learning. One thing we do know about adolescence is that it's a really great time to learn new things," she notes. "And having that incentive to get yourself up, dust yourself off, and try it all over again is invaluable. Otherwise, we might not try again and get the experience we need to actually do that learning we need to move from childhood to adulthood."

Of course, one might think that once a teen learns that a reward is not quite all it's cracked up to be, the shenanigans would stop. But the teenage reward system is not weighted in that way. In fact, new work by Bita Moghaddam, a neuroscientist at the University of

Pittsburgh, suggests that the anticipation of a reward may be even more important than the reward itself. Forget Jonathan's actual unprotected sex, which many men might agree is a pretty good reward: The possibility of the unprotected sex, the mere idea of a little bareback action, may be even more awesome than the reality.

Moghaddam and her colleagues measured brain activity in adult and adolescent rats as they took part in a simple associative learning task. Basically, when the rats heard a certain tone, they needed to poke their noses into a particular hole. If they did so, they'd be rewarded with a sugar pellet. Because the task was so simple, the rats learned how to get their sugar very, very quickly. They were highly motivated.

But as the researchers measured brain activity, they discovered a significant difference in part of the striatum—this time to a part linked to habit formation, action selection, and motivated learning. Adolescent rats showed higher activation in this area than the other rats, but only after the tone sounded and they were nose-poking for that good sugar. The activation was not linked to the tone that let them know it was time to go poking, nor to the actual reward itself. It was all about the anticipation once the nose got into that hole and anticipated that sweet, sweet treat.

"It's very interesting that this reward is directly tapping into a region that is involved with action selection and habit formation," Moghaddam says. "So it's possible that if you are doing something that is motivating and anticipate a reward, then that could influence behavior far more strongly in adolescents than in adults."

Moghaddam argues that the anticipation of rewards may explain why adolescence is such a risk period for addiction. But, once again, that inflated anticipation may be a great help to fostering motivation—and, ultimately, the learning and growth required to sync up their motivational and control systems.

Certainly, Jonathan exudes a lot of anticipatory enthusiasm about soccer. He practices for hours every day after school and on Saturdays. He goes home after practice and does drills in his backyard. He shows up to practice even when he feels sick (or hungover). And all because of the sweet, sweet anticipation of what could happen if his team does take the state championships—the collection of prestige, accolades, and, of course, girls.

GOOD IDEAS AND BAD IDEAS

I first met Vassar brain researcher Abigail Baird at a neuroscience conference in Washington, D.C., after hearing her present some research on the teen brain in a symposium about how neuroscience should shape the law. As part of her presentation, she queried the audience: "Tell me something," she said. "Do you think swimming with sharks is a good idea or a bad idea?"

The majority of the audience, composed mostly of adults, instantly yelled back at her, "Bad idea!"

If any of the adult shark pooh-pooh-ers had been having their brains scanned at that moment, scientists would have seen increased activation in the amygdala and insula—two key parts of the brain's limbic system and important inputs to the meso-cortical limbic circuit.

You may know the amygdala as the seat of the fight-or-flight response. But Baird tells me that the amygdala is responsible for the four *F*'s. "Fight and flight, everyone knows. The next *F* is feeding. And that last *F* stands for reproduction," she jokes.

The amygdala represents the things we need to stay upright, breathing and propagating the species. And, with the basal ganglia, it helps to manage important rewards. But it is also involved in processing memory and emotional reactions and attaching social salience to objects and events. Baird likens it to the brain's "burglar alarm."

"This is a part of the brain that is very survival-oriented. It's all about keeping you alive," she says. "Not so much about thinking things through."

The insula, like the amygdala, is also implicated in emotion and decision-making. While it's in close range of the amygdala, it is a little more advanced than its neighbor. Like the amygdala, it plays a key role in survival. But it does so by helping you form visceral memories about experiences—both good and bad.

"The insula gives you those gut feelings about things—you know, those instant feelings that are critical to your decision-making, to your innate sense of right and wrong," Baird says. "But it is a highly developed structure. You aren't born with these gut feelings about things. You have to learn them."

Adults can rely both on the amygdala and their insula to help inform decision-making—and you can see both regions sending important signals to the prefrontal cortex as we make decisions. But the teen brain reacts a little differently. When Baird and colleagues used fMRI to scan the brains of teenagers as they were asked a variety of "good idea or bad idea" questions, including biting a lightbulb, eating a cockroach, and jumping off a roof, they found that their insulae were not as active as the adults'. The majority of activation was occurring in the frontal lobes, where conscious thought occurs—and they were taking much, much longer than the adults to answer the questions.

"With adults, we get an answer that is very automatic and fast. But teens don't get that," says Baird. "Instead, they show a frontal lobe response. They actually think about it for a second. Because they don't have the learning to know that it's definitely a bad idea. They don't have the experience to have built an automatic response. They have to work the idea through their frontal lobes and it's just not as efficient."

In fact, they took on the order of 300 milliseconds longer than adults to work the idea through. While 300 milliseconds may not seem like a huge amount of time, Baird says that it's significant. "People don't realize that 300 milliseconds gets people killed on a regular basis," she tells me. "That's a decision to run a red light when you're driving in your car. That's a decision to take that next drink. That's a decision to drive home after taking that drink. It's plenty of time to do damage when you're talking about a dangerous situation."

While I don't have a brain scanner in my pocket, I'm curious if Jonathan will show the same lag in response that Baird saw in her study participants—especially given how he dithered on the safe sex question.

"Is it a good idea or a bad idea to swim with sharks?"

"To swim with sharks? Um . . ." he pauses. "It depends what the circumstances are, I guess."

"You didn't give me answer. What does your gut tell you? Is it a good idea or a bad idea?"

"Oh God, this is hard. I'll just say it's a good idea if you're not covered in fish blood."

I smile and then move on. "Is it a good idea or a bad idea to bite a lightbulb?"

"To bite a lightbulb? Is it a dare? Is someone paying me?"

He's not taking me very seriously, but I push on. "Can you just answer the question?"

He smirks, running his fingers through his hair. "OK, fine. It's a bad idea, I guess." He doesn't sound very convincing.

"Is it a good idea or a bad idea to jump off a roof?"

"Um, depends. How high is the roof?"

He's not being coy. His answer, he tells me when I eye him skeptically, is contingent on whether the building is more than two stories high. But, of course, as I recently learned, he does have a bit of experience with jumping off roofs into pools. Maybe we would see a little insula activation for that particular question if he were inside the fMRI machine.

Eventually, once I ask Jonathan whether eating a cockroach is a good idea or a bad idea, he replies, relatively quickly, "Yuck. OK, that seems like a bad idea." But for the most part, he responds to each of my queries with an air of cultivated cluelessness.

When I tell Baird about this conversation, she laughs. "It's kind of funny to watch. Since teens don't have the experience, they just start repeating the question back to you, adding in details, trying to draw it out, whatever, as their brains attempt to puzzle it out," she says. "And it's an awful lot like what you might see three-year-olds doing when they are trying to explain bad behavior to adults. They just really don't know the right answer. And it gets to the point where it's almost like they are making it up as they go along."

The idea, as the mother of a future teenager, is not exactly a comfort. And yet, I'm certain that I wasn't all that much different during my own rowdy adolescence.

"I'M GETTING TOO OLD FOR THIS SHIT"

It's clear that teens have a neurobiological predisposition for pushing the envelope. And studies show that this increased risk-taking continues through the teen years and well into young adulthood. Around the age of 25, the prefrontal cortex matures to the point where one is better at applying the brakes when faced with a risky decision.

Radboud University risk researcher Bernd Figner says that studies in both the neuroeconomic and the real-world behavioral spheres consistently show that we take fewer risks as we get older. And the reason for that, he argues, is twofold.

"There is a maturation of the prefrontal cortex that is happening well into young adulthood that enables us to be better at inhibiting our most influential responses—that is one important thing," he says. "But you also see these changes because you are more experienced. You now have these experiences and you start to realize that it's not always a good idea to take so many great risks. You understand the consequences better. You realize what's at stake."

So, it's not that I'm old and boring; it's just that I'm better experienced! My limbic system has picked up enough over the years to help guide good decision-making. And my frontal lobes have matured enough to actually do something with it all. It would appear this effect is not limited to suburban moms. A study that looked at risky behaviors in experienced rock climbers found that even experienced individuals tended to scale back on riskier climbs as they aged.

Gareth Jones, a researcher at Carnegie Sports Injury Clinic in Leeds, England, in collaboration with researchers at the University of Cambridge, wondered why some rock climbers are so willing to engage in risky climbs like free soloing, or climbing without ropes, while others stick to ropes and familiar rock faces. The group was curious about what separated those kind of risk-takers from your more play-it-safe types. They found that measures of self-efficacy—a personality trait that underlies how much you believe in your own abilities to accomplish a goal (as well as deal with the stresses that accompany working toward that goal)—were predictive of how risky a climber was willing to get.

The researchers recruited more than 200 active rock climbers, with 1 to 48 years of experience, from a variety of climbing

venues in Great Britain. Participants were given a special questionnaire, called the Climbing Self-Efficacy Scale, to help the
researchers understand both the participants' level of self-efficacy
and the kinds of climbing risks they usually undertook. Questions included things like "How confident are you in your
climbing abilities?" as well as what kind of climbing (soloing or
less risky types) they preferred. The researchers found that self-
efficacy—the climbers' confidence in their abilities—was significantly correlated with experience, frequency of climbing, and
the difficulty of behaviors undertaken.

"Climbers who rated as high in self-efficacy engaged in riskier
climbs—they do more climbing too," Jones says. "And, yes, they
do take additional risks, attempting harder climbs when they
have that kind of confidence in their abilities."

"That almost makes it sound like a bad thing," I say.

"Not necessarily. What we've seen is that experienced rock
climbers understand the inherent risks of the sport. And since
they are well-practiced at performing this task, they manage them
quite well," he tells me. "Climbers are quite good at mitigating
risk because they have the experience to know what they can do
and judge which kinds of climbs are within their capabilities."

But Jones and company also found another interesting trend
in their data. Age impacted how confident the climbers were in
their ability, regardless of experience. The older the climber, the
less self-efficacy he or she showed. This was even observed in
climbers who were, by all accounts, quite skilled.

"It would seem that self-efficacy is age-related. We saw that it
reduces as you get older," he told me. "There's an old saying in

climbing, 'There's old climbers and bold climbers but no old, bold climbers.' And our research suggests that is probably quite accurate."

When I asked myself if my midlife crisis in reverse might be age-related, I wasn't far off the mark. If there are no old, bold climbers, why would one expect there to be old, bold single moms? Even those of us who enjoy riskier hobbies seem to be laying off the gas as we transition from adolescence to adulthood. But is that necessarily a good thing? Figner, the risk researcher from the Netherlands, says not always.

"For adults, when you look at these typical decision-making tasks we use in the lab, people are almost too risk-averse. We use lotteries, typically, and we find that if participants would just be willing to take a few more risks, they would make a lot more money," Figner says. "Of course, whether or not it is a good thing to take a risk always will depend on the situation. But some of us might benefit from taking a few more risks every now and again."

I can't help thinking that I am one of those persons. In fact, whenever I sit flipping through TV channels on a Saturday night, I know it to be true. Alas, it would appear that having fully developed frontal lobes, a few decades of experience, and a finely tuned insula does more than just help us make more informed choices. It can also make our decision-making a bit too automatic—and lead to our mental feet riding the brakes when we might be better off using a little more gas. It can lead to us doubting our own self-efficacy, even in areas where we have ample skills and ability. And, perhaps, all that brain maturity will result in us going home with less—money, love, fun, know-how, whatever it is we value—because we can't muster up the same kind of motivation to try new things that we could when we were adolescents.

EMBRACING YOUR INNER ADOLESCENT

....

There's a pervasive idea that teens just don't think—that the disconnect between their motivational systems and their cognitive systems means that their immature brains are somehow malfunctioning. Certainly, that was something my dad often said to me when I found myself in trouble: "What were you thinking? Were you even thinking at all?!" But the neuroscience research, on the other hand, seems to suggest that teens actually think *too* much.

"Anyone who spends any time with teenagers knows that this is true. What do they spend most of their time doing? They're sitting around talking, analyzing, doing the postmortem of some social interaction in between classes at their lockers," Baird says. "All they're doing is thinking. It's just that they don't have the experience or the cognitive traction, so to speak, to help them prioritize stuff, link things together, filter out the irrelevant stuff, and make the best decisions when they're faced with risks."

So, while you may not want your average teen investing your stock portfolio for you, the average person can learn quite a bit from these young risk-takers. For example, Baird says that questioning whether perceived limits are real or self-imposed can help adults, who naturally become more risk-averse as they age, use teen risk-taking strategies to find success.

"I always think of this P!nk song where she says, 'I'm looking for a way to become the person that I dreamt of when I was 16,' " she tells me. "I think anytime we can remember what it was like to be a teenager, to think like a teenager, and truly believe that we can do anything, it helps us succeed. Adults could learn a thing or two from teens about opening themselves up to unbridled possibility."

Take Baird's question about whether eating a cockroach is a good idea or a bad idea. She says that when she sees an adult have that immediate visceral reaction to the idea—the person who is grossed out beyond words—she asks, "What's the worst thing that could happen if you eat it?"

"Of course, they say something like it could poop or leave eggs or something like that. But then I ask them to put their adult thinking caps on. I ask them, 'Could it really harm you?' and they think about it, and remember seeing someone eat a big cockroach on *Survivor* or something, and then say, 'No, it can't harm me.' But even after thinking it through, they insist that they won't eat it," she says. "This is something that becomes deep and ingrained. Now, I'm not saying that we should all be eating cockroaches. But we have a lot of ideas and decisions that become really automatic. That's your insula taking over. And I think there are a number of areas where adults could benefit from not just staying with these automatic conclusions and, like a teenager, do some extra thinking about an idea before immediately saying no."

After talking with Baird, I'm beginning to wonder if I've been relying too heavily on my insula lately. Maybe my failing self-efficacy, my apathy toward taking risks—the close intimacy my ass has formed with my couch—stems from my insula taking in a little too much information from the sanctity of suburban life. My thoughts on work and remarriage too. Maybe it's time to get some of my other brain areas involved when making decisions so that I don't miss out on the good stuff.

To that end, I ask Jonathan what he thinks an adult like me can learn from teen risk-taking behavior. I can tell he's trying hard not to roll his eyes at me. He doesn't quite succeed. "You know, it's pretty easy to be a teenager. It's one of the easiest things to be. We're old enough that we can go out and stuff, but we don't have to worry about rent or paying bills or any of that garbage. We have a lot less worries than adults do," he tells me. "Anyone can do it, really."

Oh, the teenage hubris! I don't bother to remind him that everyone who survives into adulthood actually has done it, thank you very much. He'll figure it out soon enough. But perhaps, even in his cockiness, he has a point.

Teens have the kind of motivation that allows them to try, try again, no matter what obstacles that they face. They have the kind of dopamine surges that get them out and engaged in the world— allowing them to gain important, critical experience in the process. They risk, they learn, and they grow. And they really do believe that they can do anything. Which is why, often, they do exactly that. Perhaps it's time to stop automatically listening so much to my insula—to stop saying, "I'm too old for this shit"—and to see if I can't find a way to risk a little more and finally become the adult I wanted to be at 16.

PART III

MAKING THE MOST OF RISK

LIKE MANY, I WAS RAISED ON MYTHS and fairy tales. And if there's one thing these storybook adventures would lead you to believe, it is this: Risk-takers are born, not made. You can't try to mimic the behavior of the Amelia Earharts, the Evel Knievels, or the Mark Zuckerbergs of the world. Because there is something innate and inviolate about the man or woman who risks it all for love, money, faith, knowledge, adventure, family, adrenaline, country, or [insert other type of inspiration here]. Risk-takers seem to act largely from instinct, somehow just knowing, deep down, that the risks they take will ultimately pay off. It's an archetype—but it's an archetype that's backed up by some genetic and neurobiological research.

Let's not take things too far though. It's clear that we all have a unique biological predisposition when it comes to risk. Different behavioral responses to risk are linked to different brains, particularly measurable differences in the mesocortical limbic circuitry. Different genes result in different levels of neurotransmitters and receptors in that critical risk-and-reward processing pathway. Different genders and different ages come with their own biological sway. Taken all together, these neurobiological differences mean that my perceived reality and yours may be quite different. Similarly, my response to a particular situation, and the risks involved, may be different from yours too.

But risk-taking does not occur in a vacuum. There's more to it than brain structure, hormones, age, or genetics. Mother Nature has quite a bit to say about our responses to risk, but the differences we see from person to person, from scenario to scenario, are also strongly influenced by the environment. You can never discount culture, expectation, and other outside influences in the risk-taking equation. So, yes, some people may always cotton a bit more to risks, accepting more uncertainty and danger than the rest of us, thanks to their biology. But where and when the "brakes" get applied may vary—and will depend a great deal on the situation. Which means I cannot consider only the predisposition I was born with if I'm to figure out how to choose smarter risks. I also have to take into account what the world happens to be throwing at me.

So, yes, all of us have a certain biological predisposition to risk-taking. We are greatly influenced by our genes, our neurochemicals, and our brain circuitry when we encounter uncertainty in the world. And while there will always be some factors you cannot control about the way you approach risk, there are many others that you can. Scientists and psychologists have learned quite a bit about how different environmental factors may alter one's natural affinity for risk-taking. Those factors can include your familiarity with a situation, your social group, your emotional response, your stress level, and your response to failure. Each of these has great power to change the way we perceive and pursue risks in life—as well as our ability to mitigate the gravity of risk when we do engage. And these are all factors that, with the right knowledge and self-awareness, we can manage and control. This holds true for those who are naturally inclined to push the envelope and for those who try to avoid risks at all costs.

And, as I'm learning, it's the combination of these two things—your innate predisposition to risk-taking and the way you navigate your environment—that provides the key to understanding how to best leverage risk to find more success in life. And by better understanding the interaction of the two, you hold the power to take charge and make risk work to your best advantage.

Chapter Seven

....

RISK AND PREPARATION

AT FIRST GLANCE, any hard-core rock climber—which I would define as someone who ascends steep peaks in Yosemite as opposed to just fooling around in their local climbing gym—may seem like a risk-taker. But outdoor adventurer Steph Davis takes risk-taking to a whole nother level.

Davis is a world-renowned rock climber—but that's just a start. She is also a top building-antenna-span-and-earth (BASE) jumper. Basically, she's known for climbing up really high, really steep cliffs without a rope and then jumping off with a parachute. She's remarkably good at it, too. Davis is the first woman to have successfully free-climbed Salathé Wall on El Capitan, Yosemite National Park's towering (and somewhat terrifying) rock monolith. She's one of the few women climbers to free solo—that is, climb without the benefit of a partner, rope, or anchoring devices—on some tough, steep, and serious walls. You can find her successful free solo of Pervertical Sanctuary, a 1,000-plus-foot granite wall on Colorado's Long Peak, recorded for posterity on YouTube. But I warn you, it's not for the faint of heart. Just watching her scale this mammoth rock face sans ropes made me sweat a little. OK, a lot.

Davis has been sponsored by legendary outdoor companies like Patagonia, prAna, and Backcountry. (Once upon a time, she was also sponsored by Clif Bar, but it recently dropped her contract after stating she was one of a group of extreme athletes who "are pushing boundaries and taking the element of risk to a place where we as a company are no longer willing to go.") She leaps from airplanes, helicopters, hot-air balloons, and towering cliffs wearing a wing suit, a special jumpsuit that mimics the body style of a flying squirrel or bat to increase lift and flying time. She is an environmentalist and passionate vegan. She follows the philosophies of Buddha and Sufi—and, as a literature major, she reads like it is going out of style. She's trained both as a jump master and a classical pianist. She is an author and a coveted public speaker. Her book and blog, both titled *High Infatuation,* are a favorite among outdoor enthusiasts. She has made a career—and a life—based on the things she loves to do. It's more than fair to say that Steph Davis is a risk-taker. I don't believe there's much that she couldn't do if she put her mind to it. She really is a total badass, admirably brave and unabashedly alive.

She is also a young widow.

In August 2013, Davis was BASE jumping in the Dolomites, part of Italy's northern Alps, with her husband, BASE jumping legend Mario Richard. After making a series of wingsuit flights, Davis jumped from Sasso Pordoi, the so-called terrace of the Dolomites, with Richard taking off only moments behind her. Davis landed successfully. Her husband, however, did not. Richard hit the rocks with enough force during his descent, according to reports, that "rescue operations were in vain."

It would be easy to say that many risk-takers, especially those who enjoy the most extreme of extreme sports, simply don't understand the full consequences of their favorite pastimes. That they haven't connected that a faulty parachute or unpredictable winds could result in severe injury or death. As you watch them perform death-defying feats, you tell yourself that they are a little crazy— they must overestimate the odds and put too much faith in their own invincibility. They just haven't thought it through. How else can you explain how they do what they do? How else can you explain *why* they do what they do?

Davis is different. She has always been mindful about the chances she takes. She understands the risks involved in her chosen sports in a very personal way—perhaps the most personal way. The probabilities of negative outcomes are very real for her. Those potential outcomes have taken friends from her. They've taken the love of her life.

Yet, less than two weeks after her husband's death, Davis was BASE jumping again.

"It was really emotional, but I needed to do it," she tells me, her face tightening with sadness as she tries to explain. "BASE jumping is something I love so much. And so did Mario. It's something that was so special to both of us. I didn't know how it was going to be, whether it was going to feel good to me anymore, how I was going to be doing it. But I felt like I had to find out."

Yes, Davis knows the risks involved with climbing and jumping. She understands the uncertainty and the danger all too well. But she feels she can handle those risks. She holds a healthy respect for the process and the work involved in extreme sports. Likewise, for the equipment and the people she relies on as she undertakes those endeavors. But, perhaps most important, she has a deep respect for the potential outcomes. She understands, acknowledges, and accepts them as being part of a sport that has given her "more joy and grief than anything, really."

And, wouldn't you know it, a big part of that respect, for Davis and other successful risk-takers, is being prepared for whatever may come.

GETTING FAMILIAR WITH RISK

They say that familiarity breeds contempt. But it also helps determine whether a person is willing to take a risk or not. Sarah Helfinstein, the University of Texas at Austin researcher who studies risk and decision-making, wondered what the difference was between the kinds of risks that we, as a society or a group, decidedly encourage and those that we shun. She found that familiarity, particularly familiarity with a certain pursuit thanks to the predilections of your social circle, plays a big part in what risks we find acceptable.

Helfinstein used the Domain-Specific Risk-Taking (DOSPERT) scale, a popular psychometric measure that examines risk in financial, health and safety, recreational, ethical, and social domains. Basically, participants are presented with different scenarios in those different realms of decision-making and asked to rate the likelihood that they would take part in such activities. Scenarios include things like having an affair with a married person, going skydiving over the weekend, and disagreeing with your boss in a big meeting at work. Helfinstein extended the scale. After asking study participants how likely they were to partake in the various activities, she included these follow-up questions: "Do you know many people who have engaged in this kind of scenario?" "How likely would you be to encourage a loved one to engage in this scenario?" "How much benefit would you derive from this scenario?" "What would be the likelihood of a negative occurrence if you participated—and what would be the cost if that outcome happened?"

By summing all the different answers, Helfinstein found a striking result. "It was a pretty whopping effect of familiarity," she says. "Basically, we found that the more people you know who are engaging in a particular activity, the more likely you are willing to engage in it too. And that's even if you don't think it's actually a good thing to do."

To follow up on those results, Helfinstein designed a questionnaire study. She gave participants abstract risk scenarios based on those DOSPERT situations—things that they have likely encountered in real life—and then offered statistical information about how many people engage in such activities. She then asked how willing each participant would be to engage—as well as encourage someone else to do it after seeing those numbers. When people read that everybody was doing it, whether it was hopping into bed with married folks or going skydiving, they were more likely to say they would partake themselves.

"It would seem that what environment you happen to be in hugely drives your willingness to engage in risk. Much more so than the mathematical features of risk that so many neuroeconomists talk about," she says. Familiarity has some serious pull, both in terms of what your peers are doing and in what you experience day in and day out in your natural environment. It makes more than a little sense. I think about the people I knew who grew up in Small Town, U.S.A. To them, the idea of taking the subway in New York City is tantamount to begging for an assault. They would rather throw cash away on a cab ride or walk the entirety of Manhattan in the rain than risk a mugging on the subway. My city slicker compadres, on the other hand, think nothing of taking the train. They don't understand what country folk are making such a fuss about. But I have a feeling they might find navigating some of those poorly marked backcountry roads distressing. What you know, what you are familiar with, is always going to affect how you perceive any risks you may be facing. It helps you to put them in context—and push you in one direction or another.

Of course, familiarity isn't all there is to it when you are talking risk perception. Look at Davis. While familiarity and a crowd may explain part of the reason she originally got into skydiving and BASE jumping—she just happened to be hanging out with a lot of climbers who also had a penchant for jumping when she first gave it a go—it doesn't explain her love of climbing. She wasn't that four-year-old kid you see ripping across the climbing wall at the indoor gym. She spent most of her high school years perched over a piano, not on a cliff. In fact, she didn't even start climbing until she was in college. And, at first, it was a lark, the acceptance of an unfamiliar invitation. Yet somehow, despite that lack of familiarity, that first experience transformed into a life-long passion.

So, yes, while familiarity is important, you aren't always going to take a risk just because everyone else is doing it. But while familiarity certainly isn't the be-all and end-all of risk perception, it is something that has more power than you realize. It has enough oomph to help push you toward a risk you might not have considered otherwise.

PRACTICE MAKES . . .

So, what happens once you become familiar with a particular pastime, either through your friends, your family, or your own behavioral habits? Well, in theory, you start participating in it—and participating means practice. Lots and lots of practice. And then, with even more practice, you start to get better. And then, with significantly more practice, on the order of years or more, you will theoretically become an expert.

When Davis was in high school, she would spend hours upon hours practicing the piano. Before she started scaling vertical walls, she had mastered scales on the ivories. And she had to put in a serious amount of time to do that. Once Davis started climbing, during college, she didn't just jump up on a hard rock face one day on a whim and try to master it. Each climbing success took considerable effort and commitment.

Davis was the first woman to successfully free-climb Free Rider, a grueling route along El Capitan's Salathé Wall. But she couldn't do so on her first try, despite years of climbing experience under her belt. Rather, she spent the better part of two seasons learning its quirks, practicing her moves, and getting ready to make her solo attempt.

"I feel like people only see the outcome; they don't see all the work that goes into getting ready for a big climb," she says, curling up in a cozy armchair at her house in Moab, Utah. "I worked on Free Rider a lot. When I wasn't there working on it, I was back home in Moab doing things to get ready to go back and work on it some more. I was going bouldering a lot, and running, and getting more fit. Because, in my mind, I wanted to go back and keep trying it."

All that practice is key—no matter if you are playing the piano or climbing a big rock face. But you have to practice in the right way. Erik Dane, a professor of business at Rice University who studies decision-making, says that to get the most benefit, you have to partake in something called "deliberate practice."

"You really need to practice at the edge of your performance ability. And that means you are going to be continually failing but getting right back up and trying again," he says. "Deliberate practice is the classic model for getting really good at something, working to the point where you can eventually gain expertise. And if you think of the burgeoning violinist, they select a very tricky passage. And they work on that passage, failing over and over again, until they just get it. Working right around the edge really helps you learn and progress."

And that's just how Davis works when she takes on a new climbing "project." She makes sure to practice at the edge. Remember what Michael Frank, the Brown University neuroscientist, said about rock climbing: "Sticking with the status quo can make it hard to learn and improve at anything . . . if you don't rely on risk and try harder courses, you're never going to become a better rock climber." Risk-taking is integral to learning. You have to push your boundaries and take a few risks if you want to improve at a given task.

"Free-climbing is a lot like a piano piece or a dance. You have to try it and practice it so many times. You could fail so many times because you took a fall. But you keep at it, and then, one day, you do it. You've succeeded. It's just like anything that needs to be rehearsed quite a bit in order to be perfected," Davis says. "For me, it's just like piano. You pick something too hard. You practice, practice, practice. And, eventually, you can do it. And it's such an amazing feeling when you finally do."

As you might have guessed, that art of deliberate practice confers some amazing benefits to the brain. And those changes result in both a certain level of automaticity in behavior as well as the ability to focus on important, as opposed to distracting, risk factors as you are making decisions.

First of all, it sharpens your motor skills. Scott Grafton, a neuroscientist who directs the Action Lab at the University of California, Santa Barbara, has found that practice helps the brain organize movement into goal-oriented action. And the representations that the mind creates during practice make all the difference when it comes to successfully planning movements. It's why someone like Davis can look inside a rock crack and immediately understand exactly the right way to move her hand so that she can get a solid grip and move herself up. It just comes effortlessly. And it's why someone like me can look at the same crack and not even realize there might be a handhold in there at all. I just don't have the experience to make those kinds of connections between my body and the world.

People talk a lot about muscle memory. But, of course, muscles don't have memories—they rely on signals from our brains to work optimally. Extended practice activates a network in the brain called the action-observation network—a circuit involving the motor cortex (the region of the brain responsible for movement), temporal cortex (the part of the brain involved with memory and processing sensory input), and frontal cortex (the seat of executive control and function)—giving you a boost in how your brain communicates with the rest of your body. Activating this network means you can mentally rehearse movements, which prepares you for when it comes time to actually execute them. You can learn better from observation of others' movement since you have the experience to put it in context. And, perhaps most important, harnessing the action-observation network through practice allows you to break down movement into digestible "chunks," so, over time, more complicated routines become easier to learn—and the movements within them become very automatic.

According to Grafton, thinking too much can actually get in the way when we are trying to accomplish physical goals—and this is because the brain's motor systems work at speeds much faster than our higher-level cognitive ones. "The speed at which we talk, at which we think verbally is no better than an old 56k modem dial-up," he tells me. "If you think about how fast things are going when you make a golf swing, or hit a baseball, or do some gymnastics, you just can't think and expect to not interfere with your body. As soon as you think about it, and try to make adjustments on the fly, you'll see your performance degenerate."

Practice also makes your brain work more efficiently. Nathalie Picard, a neurobiologist at the University of Pittsburgh, wondered how long-term training on a simple movement task might modify activity in the motor cortex. She and her colleagues decided to totally commit to looking at those associated changes. Over several years, the group trained monkeys on a sequence of short, simple movements. Monkeys were either visually guided in making them, cued by a computer on where to reach and touch, or they had to use their own memory to remember the sequence, internally generating the routine without help from the outside world.

When Picard and her colleagues looked at the motor cortices of the animals, they found something interesting. In terms of basic activity, there was no difference between animals that were cued versus those that had to do the sequence by memory. The same number of neurons fired at about the same rate. What was different was the metabolic activity in this brain region. After extended practice, the monkeys internally guiding the movements required less metabolic activity than those being visually guided. The brain required less energy to complete the task after practice, perhaps through greater synchrony of sensory input or more effective synapses. Which means all that practice is making your brain much, much more efficient.

It's likely that this sort of practice-induced brain efficiency extends beyond the motor cortex—not to mention beyond simple athletics. Researchers at University College London found that experienced taxi drivers, who practice navigating the complex streets and alleyways of the busy city each and every day, show dramatic differences in the gray matter volume of their hippocampi, an area of the brain involved with memory. Moreover, the greater their navigation experience, the greater the volume in their right posterior hippocampus, the part involved with spatial memory.

Researchers at the Karolinska Institute in Sweden found that extensive piano practice strengthens fiber tracts, or neural pathways, in the brain by increasing the amount of myelin. You can think of myelin as a sort of insulation—and the more of it that is wrapped around the neural circuits, the faster the connected brain regions can communicate. Individuals who have been practicing the piano since childhood have hardier, speedier connections in the frontal cortex than those who have not. Other studies have shown that practice reduces demands on the frontoparietal area of the brain, an area linked to working memory, making tasks less effortful and more automatic.

These are only a few of the changes in the brain that have been demonstrated as individuals work toward expertise. Depending on the task at hand and the type of practice, there are likely many, many others. Taken together, all that practice does more than just make perfect. It makes for stronger action representations and strong, intentional movement. It makes for reduced metabolic needs. It makes for decreased effort and more automaticity—and a strong platform for new learning.

TALKING ABOUT SOME INTUITION

You may be wondering why more automaticity is such a good thing. After all, we already said that you need your gas, that increased basal ganglia activity, and your brakes, that prefrontal regulator, working together to make optimal decisions. So why would easing up on the brakes be any kind of benefit if you are about to climb a 1,000-foot wall without safety equipment? How is it going to help you?

It's a matter of resource allocation. If you have only so much cognitive effort to go around, you want to make sure it's focused on the right variables in your risk equation. You want to make sure your brain and body are working in a highly efficient state. You want to be able to rely on your fast-thinking systems so that your cognitive effort can deal with something other than the basics. You want to maximize attention and working memory all while regulating stress. And these are all things that can improve performance, even in risky situations.

"If you have practiced enough that you are an expert in a particular field, you have a lot of information about that field on hand.

You can anticipate what comes next, what you need to do, the best way to respond to a situation, and so on," says Michael Posner, a pioneering neuroscientist who has been studying attention at the University of Oregon for decades. "That means you can deal with things in your field that people without that expertise can't. It allows you to deploy your attention faster and in a different way."

And it can allow you to approach your decision-making with some unconscious intuition. What exactly is intuition? Scientifically speaking, it's simply synchronizing your current decision-making situation with past experience. But it doesn't require your conscious-level cognitive resources to do so.

"People want to talk about intuition like it's some kind of mystical or religious thing," Rice University's Dane says, chuckling. "From a scientific standpoint, however, it's a pattern-matching process. You are essentially mapping all the experiences you've accrued to the situation at hand—and it's happening at a very unconscious, automatic level. Often, you aren't even aware of why or how you started moving toward a particular decision."

So, we aren't necessarily aware of a lot of things that are influencing our decisions. J. David Creswell, director of Carnegie Mellon University's Health and Human Performance Laboratory, wondered how unconscious processing—the very stuff of which intuitions are made—might influence decision-making on a task. He, along with former student James Bursley, recruited 27 students to have their brains scanned while making a decision about cars and other consumer items. First, participants were given information about the various products. For the car, for example, they were offered 12 attributes for 1.75 seconds each about each choice:

things like "Car A has leather seats," and "Car B has bad gas mileage." Each car had a different distribution of positive and negative attributes, with one showing a much higher number of positive than negative ones—making it the optimal choice.

After getting educated on the products in question, the participants were asked to do one of three things: rate the various options based on their attributes immediately; look at a fixation cross for two minutes and then do their ratings; or do a distractor task—in this case, watch a series of digits presented on the screen and click a button if a digit was already presented two numbers back—for two minutes and then rate the items in question.

Creswell and Bursley found something interesting. As the participants were doing all that learning, activity ramped up in both the prefrontal and visual cortices—areas that are important for both learning and decision-making. But those areas were then reactivated during the distractor task, even though they weren't needed. This, the researchers argue, means that these regions were still unconsciously working on making a good decision even while the brain was busy doing something else. In fact, the more these areas were reactivated during the distractor task, the better the participants did on their ratings of the different cars afterward. They were able to make better, smarter decisions than those who weren't distracted. All that unconscious processing was giving the participants a decision-making boost.

Dane says that unconscious processing is an important part of intuition. But he tells me that he thinks people make even better intuitive decisions when they have a strong background in a given area. "Practice, experiences—these produce intuitions. But expertise helps produce really effective intuitions," he says. "People with advanced skills and performance abilities within a given domain tend to have much more accurate intuitions. This is because they have a richer set of knowledge, which allows more effective pattern matching."

So, as you might imagine, all that experience, accrued from practice, would be a big help. Expertise would be even better. But Creswell and Bursley's study did not look at that particular factor.

To get a better handle on how practice and expertise may interact in unconscious decision-making, I ask Bursley, "If I know a lot about a certain area—say, I'm a car nut or I've been doing a lot of research about the kind of car I'm going to buy—does that make the unconscious processing more effective? Will I make better decisions?"

"Probably. There have been a lot of studies that have looked at expertise and decision-making. And the general message is that when you have that background in an area, you get an even bigger boost from unconscious processing than if you don't know anything about it or are just moderately familiar with something," he tells me. "Experience matters."

"So, how might something like unconscious processing help with a risky decision?" I ask. "Do you think it helps mitigate some of that risk?"

"I don't know that anyone has looked at that directly," Bursley says. "But if I were to speculate, I think it would help quite a bit. Human brains have developed this capacity to unconsciously process important information that helps us make decisions. And it wouldn't surprise me if this offline processing serves some evolutionary purpose to help us move out of situations that are risky and solve problems that are really relevant to survival."

Historically, however, intuitive decisions have been seen as less than optimal. Those so-called fast-thinking systems can often lead you astray. And, when significant risk is involved, I feel like you'd want something pretty dependable. Can intuition really help us make better decisions?

Rice University's Dane says it depends. Intuition can be a help or a hindrance—you can't say which until you know the specifics.

"As a general rule, in tasks that are concerned with math or logic, in tasks that can be broken down into a series of concrete steps, we see that people do better when they approach them analytically," he says. "In contrast, what we've seen is that when tasks are less structured, less conducive to a mathematical approach, intuition has a lot going for it. It can lead you to a good decision really quickly, whereas analyzing the problem for a while might not get you to a better or a safer place."

"So, with so many caveats, when should you trust your intuition?" I ask Dane.

"That's a very good question—and it's still an open research question. Some will tell you it depends on the task. Others say it depends on your expertise. But it probably depends on some kind of interaction between the two," he says. "Here's what it shouldn't depend on: some kind of fly-by-the-seat-of-your-pants style. Some people are more inclined to make intuitive decisions; others are more analytical and rational. But the truth is, you can be both. And it can be a benefit to be both provided you have the knowledge and skills to really understand all the facets of a particular decision."

Steph Davis certainly relies on her intuition when it comes to deciding whether or not to make a BASE jump—which, one could easily argue, is not a very mathy kind of situation. When I ask her what helps her determine whether she'll jump, she tells me that in the BASE jumping world, she's actually considered quite conservative in her choices.

"There are a lot of jumps I won't do. If it doesn't look right, if it doesn't feel right, or I just don't like it, I'll always walk down," she says, sipping some tea.

"There are so many factors you need to think about. Some jumps are a lot more technical than others. So you have to consider the kind of cliff it is, whether it's bulging or undercut, or whether there's something you have to jump over. Then there's the landing. It could be a really small place or hard to get into. If you don't fly your parachute perfectly, you might run into a tree or rock," she explains.

This is all starting to sound pretty analytical—a critical evaluation of the factors based on expert knowledge and past experience. But as she talks more about making a decision to jump, I realize that her experience means most of these determinations are all but automatic. She has enough time and enough practice to quickly, effectively, and unconsciously grok the information required to make a good decision. And the sum result is her intuition about the jump.

"It comes down to whether I feel good or bad about the jump. And if I feel bad enough, I'm not going to do it. I won't force myself," she says. "I'm going to trust myself, and I'm going to walk away."

OPENING THE DOOR

....

Some might be surprised that after the death of her husband, Davis not only returned to BASE jumping but also returned to the sport so quickly. "I look at risk as opening a door. And there are some doors I don't want to open. There are some roads I'm not interested in going down," she says.

It surprises me, given that she seems so fearless, that there are some risks she won't take. Davis tells me about two climbing trips to Pakistan in 1998 and 2000. "I loved it. I loved the culture, the people, the traveling, the climbing, and the mountains," she said. "I wanted to go back so badly."

She'd planned to do just that—she'd even received a grant to fund the trip. But the journey was scheduled not long after 9/11. And when a climbing acquaintance disappeared near the area where she planned to climb, never to be heard from again, she decided to cancel the trip.

"The more I thought about it, the more I realized that going back was a door that could result in me sitting in some cement hut in Pakistan with a knife at my throat. Nothing is worth that. I don't ever want to open that door," she says. "That outcome is unacceptable to me."

But free soloing and BASE jumping are different. "I love [both] so much. And the idea of hitting the ground when I jump off a cliff, while I don't want it to happen and am going to do whatever I can to make sure it doesn't happen, is an acceptable outcome to me. I know it's a possibility. But it's a risk I'm willing to take so I can keep doing what I love."

I like Davis's metaphor about risk simply being about opening a door. Mitigating risk is about understanding the dangers, accepting the uncertainty, and then getting a handle on the potential outcomes. Only then can you decide whether those potential outcomes are acceptable to you.

Given the research, it's clear that familiarity, whether received through your peers' experience or your own, is something that makes you aware that the door exists, that what's behind that door may be a possibility for you. Familiarity changes the way you perceive the risks involved—it makes you open, more comfortable, and more willing to explore. Experience (developed with a commitment to deliberate practice), on the other hand, helps you determine whether it's a door you want to go through. It changes the way your brain approaches the decision, reallocating attention and other cognitive resources, so you can both understand and mitigate the risks involved. It helps sync up your gas and your brakes, so to speak, so you can rely on more informed intuition to guide you. And, taken together, all else being equal, that experience gleaned from deliberate practice will lead you to more optimal decisions when faced with risks.

Familiarity is what helps you decide whether or not to open the door. The experience you've gained from practice is what helps you determine whether it makes sense to hit the gas and head on through it. I know it sounds a bit like good, old-fashioned common sense. But it's good, old-fashioned common sense that's been validated in the laboratory. Without both familiarity and experience, it would be impossible to understand what the risks are in any given decision—and whether they are worth taking. So, before you decide to take a risk in a particular arena, it pays to practice, to learn, to gain all that vital experience, so that your intuition and unconscious processing systems are working for you, rather than against you.

Chapter Eight

....

RISK AND CONNECTION

CERTAIN WORDS ARE OFTEN USED to describe the traditional military officer's wife: conservative, demure, old-fashioned, patriotic, self-sacrificing. Think sweater sets and pearls—and a woman with an unflinching devotion to God, country, community, and family. She's the officer's perfect helpmate, taking care of hearth and home without complaint as her husband carries out his duties. She is tough yet accommodating. And she holds true to the military's values and traditions, both in times of war and peace.

One thing a traditional officer's spouse is *not?* A risk-taker. Not only do military spouses shy away from physical danger as much as possible, but they also avoid shaking things up in the social arena. As we've learned, breaking stereotypes and pushing social boundaries are also risky propositions. And those are two things that military spouses are never, ever supposed to do.

Certainly, my description is a stereotype. But the stereotype exists for a reason. Officer's wives, especially those of high-ranking officers, can be a bit of a type. They are quite a bit like June Cleaver, come to think of it—just with longer hair, an American flag sweater, and a full volunteer calendar. Which is why many are surprised that Kristina Kaufmann, executive director of the Code of Support Foundation, a nonprofit focused on bridging the gap between the military and the civilian worlds to support service members and their families, was the wife of a lieutenant colonel who commanded a battalion during the war in Iraq.

Maybe it's her degree from the University of California, Berkeley. Very few graduates from this liberal school—known more for radical protests than for traditional patriotism—go on to military-related vocations. Perhaps it's her unreserved and direct manner. Kaufmann is definitely not afraid to speak her mind (and I doubt anyone has ever referred to her as being even in the neighborhood of "demure"). It may be the fact that she married later in life, or that she is childless, by choice, or that she is of the more liberal persuasion. Or, you know, it may have something to do with the fact that she's always racing around on her motorcycle. Now that she works on Washington, D.C.'s conservative Capitol Hill, more than a few folks have seen her do a quick change from her pink and black leathers into a business suit and heels, minutes before heading into a meeting with senators and other key lawmakers. It's a sight, I'm told.

Kaufmann is definitely a risk-taker. And she would be the first to tell you that she's never been your more traditional military spouse. She admitted as much in a controversial editorial in the

Washington Post back in 2009 about how the U.S. Army was failing its families. She wrote that the Army was putting too much of a burden on the military community after eight years of war, and that too many spouses were feeling "embittered, powerless and disconnected from the Army in which we and our husbands serve." She tells me that she was compelled to share the stories of the families she'd seen fall prey to domestic violence, extreme stress, mental illness, and suicide despite tremendous community pressure to remain silent.

"I definitely understood that I wasn't supposed to be speaking out. It was a serious breach of protocol, to say the least. Time and time again, as I tried to bring up these issues, and I tried for years, I was told there was a 'right' way to handle them. And the 'right' way did not include an op-ed in the *Washington Post*," she tells me. "But it just got to the point where nothing was happening. Nothing was changing even though so many people were struggling. And I thought to myself, if I don't say something, if I don't bring attention to all these issues that military families are facing, I'm going to regret it for the rest of my life."

And so, though she worried about the possibility of backlash against her husband from the higher-ups, she wrote the piece. It took her months, and multiple iterations, before it was published. If she was going to take such a risk, she says she was damned well going to get it right. And it seems that she did. Her editorial went viral, both in the military and civilian communities. Soon, multiple military, government, and nonprofit agencies were asking her to write more, collaborate, and find new ways to help serve the military community.

But she got a mix of reactions to the op-ed. "The majority of people who reached out to me thanked me for speaking up. But I also got some pushback," she says. "But it's funny—in terms of the pushback, no one really disagreed with what I said. In fact, they agreed with me. They just made it clear that I shouldn't have said it in the *Washington Post.*"

Kaufmann's detractors agreed with her opinions, but they didn't cotton to her sharing them in such a public forum. She had violated the unspoken rules of the military community by publishing such an editorial. A good military spouse does not bite the hand that feeds her family. If changes are necessary, she works from within—using standard operating procedures. She knows to keep Army issues separate from family issues. And she certainly doesn't air the Army's dirty laundry in one of the most widely circulated newspapers in the world.

Risks are not limited to the physical realms. The popular Domain-Specific Risk-Taking (DOSPERT) scale looks beyond safety and recreation, recognizing that there is a lot to lose when you try to buck your social system. Think of the potential costs of having an affair with your neighbor's husband, standing up to your boss at work, or, as Kaufmann did, publishing an editorial that criticized the way the Army was doing business. Humans are naturally social creatures—and taking such risks can come at a high price, for both ourselves and those closest to us. So it's probably little surprise that scientists are learning that our social groups have the power to influence how, where, when, and why we take risks.

TEENS AND PEER PRESSURE

....

Kaufmann will tell you that she has always been a bit of a boundary pusher. "You should have seen me as a teenager!" she says, laughing. "Best way to get me to do something was to tell me I couldn't or shouldn't."

And, certainly, we've learned quite a bit about why the teenage brain's neurobiological setup can lead to excessive risk-taking. But, beyond biology, another important factor to consider in teen risk-taking is peer pressure. Adolescents, because of their lack of experience, will often follow their friends both in and out of trouble. Talk to any public health official and they will tell you that the data are clear: Teens are more likely to take drugs, crash their cars, or commit a crime when in a group. Having the wrong friends can definitely lead you astray. When I think back to my own most stupid moments during my teen years, I can't help realizing that I was almost always running with a crowd.

Most teens won't admit how much influence their friends have when it comes to risky business. Of course, it's possible they aren't even aware of it—teenagers aren't cursed with too much self-awareness, after all. Temple University neuroscientist Laurence Steinberg has identified the underlying brain processes that make teens so susceptible to peer influence.

Steinberg and his colleague Jason Chein used fMRI to scan adolescents, young adults, and adults as they played a simulated driving game. The goal was simple: to reach the end of a driving course as quickly as possible. If study participants managed to do so under a certain time, they would be awarded some cash. As on most driving tracks, participants had to navigate various intersections, choosing whether to run through a yellow light, putting them at risk for a collision with another vehicle, or to stop and wait for the light to change, risking a longer course time.

When teenagers did the task by themselves, they showed similar driving styles and brain activation patterns to the adults'. But when they were told that their friends would be watching their performance, the teens not only took a greater number of risks, running more yellow lights, but also showed greater activation in areas of the brain involved with reward processing. Chein says the result was not a matter of distraction; if it were, the researchers would have seen changes in activation in the frontal lobes. Rather, he and Steinberg suggest, teens really tune into the potential upsides of a risky decision. The teens were evaluating the risks as they drove just fine—but adding a social element made the anticipation of the reward, making that money, that much greater. And that resulted in them making poorer decisions in order to beat the clock. It's possible that the heightened reward activation seen in so many teen studies is amplified even more by social context.

It's a compelling idea. After all, the social stuff is a huge part of teenage life. It's a reward in itself—so it makes sense that it would influence adolescents as they face risky decisions. But Vassar researcher Abigail Baird, the one who asked teens about swimming with sharks and biting lightbulbs, argues that it is a mistake to mark all peer pressure as "bad"—it's throwing the baby out with the bathwater.

Baird's lab also conducted a peer pressure experiment. She and her colleagues recruited seventh- and eighth-grade girls and scanned them in an fMRI while they answered some opinion questions regarding music, movies, television shows, and other teenage kind of stuff on a website. In the first trial, the researchers told the teens that it was just a dry run—they would not be logged into the website and no one would see their answers. But the second time around, they would be logged into a live website and teens in the area, perhaps even teens that they go to school with, could see their answers.

"We gave them pretty basic questions. You know, what kind of music they liked or what kind of television shows they liked. It was not hard. And when they thought they were just practicing and no one could see what they were writing, the activity in their brains looked exactly like that in adult brains. They were using their prefrontal cortexes," Baird tells me. "But when they had the perception that someone their age *might* see something they were saying in the second go-around, that all changed. We saw a ton of activity in their insula and amygdala. They were on guard and not so much thinking about their answers as *feeling* about their answers."

Baird says this is important. Without adult experience, it can be hard to understand the subtleties of the world—and how they should be influencing your decision. Learning to listen to your intuition is important. And it would appear that the social environment is what helps teens to inform intuition before they get the requisite experience.

"We always talk about peer pressure and drugs and sex and other bad behaviors. There's a whole literature on how we can train kids to resist peer pressure. But that leaves out an important part of teen social behavior. We don't talk about the positive aspects of social understanding and peer pressure," she says. "Because, you know, if all of your friends are going to college and do not shoplift, well, guess what? Your odds of behaving in a similar way are pretty good. And that's a good thing."

Baird refers back to her research about whether swimming with sharks or biting a lightbulb are good or bad ideas—which suggests teens take longer to answer those questions (and show all that frontal lobe activation) because they don't have the experience to help make their responses automatic. She argues that one way that adolescents figure out how to navigate new situations when they lack that important experience is to look to their friends.

"We evolved to learn from our peers—especially those who are a little older and more experienced," she says. "That way we can learn from them and avoid mistakes. You see the same thing in really young kids in how they learn from their older siblings by emulating them. Teens are doing the same thing. They are just looking at their friends to see how they should be doing things."

Baird, unlike many who study teen risk-taking, believes that teens have some hard-core neurobiology dedicated to understanding their social sphere. "This is the stuff that helps you focus on the life lessons and priorities you need to learn to succeed as an adult in your environment," she says. "Evolution did not have heroin or bath salts in mind when it set up the brain this way. So, I think, asking a teen to 'resist' peer pressure is asking them to fight their neurobiology and evolution. Two things that I would not want to try to beat."

The social environment—group cohesion—is important. Much in the same way primates need a social group to help them survive the wild, teens need their social group to survive their own version of the jungle: middle and high school. Being aware of— and responding appropriately to—the social environment, in many ways, is critical not only to survival but also to success.

GROUPTHINK

The work of Temple University's Laurence Steinberg suggests that adults aren't as susceptible as teens to peer influence. Adults tend to perform the same on the driving task whether they think someone else is watching or not. But does that mean a more developed frontal lobe protects you from social influence? Alas, as anyone who has worked a little too hard to try to impress one's work team or book club knows, it does not. Even as adults, we put a lot of stock in what our friends, family, and co-workers have to say about what's risky and what's not. Sometimes, too much stock. According to Ruth Murray-Webster, a corporate risk consultant and co-author of *Understanding and Managing Group Risk Attitude,* people are often susceptible to groupthink when they consider risks.

"Groupthink," as originally described by Yale University psychologist Irving Janis, is "a mode of thinking that people engage in when they are deeply involved in a cohesive group, when the members' strivings for unanimity override their motivation to realistically appraise alternative courses of action." Simply stated, it's when the beliefs and attitudes of your social group are given too much weight in your decision-making process.

Janis got into this line of research by trying to understand some big government fiascoes. Why did the U.S. government overlook intelligence that Japan was about to attack Pearl Harbor? How did we allow the Vietnam War to escalate? And how on earth did the Bay of Pigs invasion ever get the green light? There was a common thread in these decisions: a core group of decision-makers who were more alike than not, and who believed in their own superior morality and invulnerability. Because of this kind of groupthink, the group did not consider all the variables involved with these important decisions. They actively censored potential detractors, and in doing so, made biased decisions that led to costly strategic failures. But groupthink isn't limited to government debacles. Janis's research suggests that any tight-knit group may have a tendency toward faulty decision-making. And Murray-Webster says that when group members are similar in ideology and insulated from alternative ideas, they are not as good at determining when a risk is worth taking.

"We see that groupthink can work both ways, both in terms of making organizations take more risks, as Janis saw in his work, or in influencing the group to take less risks," Murray-Webster says. "My experience is that people tend to play 'follow the leader,' and look to the attitudes of the most powerful person in the group when making a decision. That has massive influence. And if that person is pushing for big risks, the group will follow. If that person is more risk-averse, the group will be more cautious."

The military community, especially those traditional military spouses, would make an excellent case study for groupthink. They are people who tend to share a very similar belief system. They are insulated from the civilian world just by the nature of their spouses' vocation. And they have been told, time and again, that tradition and service trumps all. If Kaufmann had asked a group of high-ranking officers' spouses to contribute to her *Washington Post* op-ed, I doubt it ever would have been written, let alone published. The group likely would have chosen to avoid the risk altogether. But, as a bit of an outsider, Kaufmann could see the value of ignoring the hive mind and saying her piece.

"I think I had the benefit of an objective eye. I didn't marry into the military until I was 30. Many of the more senior wives had grown up in the military community. That's all they had ever known," Kaufmann says. "But I had my own friends, my own profession, my own world outside the military. So it wasn't like it was the only life I had ever known and I was totally indoctrinated to it."

Murray-Webster often encounters different varieties of groupthink when she consults with different organizations—and she says that it can happen in any closely affiliated group. Families, neighborhoods, church groups, schools, or even your friendly neighborhood Boy Scout troops may not be immune. But, she argues, the negative influence involved with groupthink can be held at bay by just thinking outside the group.

"Filtration is key. So having a neutral facilitator to help you work through a risky decision, and help make sure you are considering the alternatives, is very helpful," she says. "But what we've also seen is that being open to challenge is really vital. To encourage transparency and allow people to address the group with any misgivings or challenges so they can be fully considered."

It's not unlike what researcher Baird had to say about adults relying on their insulae when asked "good idea or bad idea" questions. When you're faced with a risky decision, especially one that is influenced by group dynamics, it pays to step away from any automatic conclusions and to ask yourself, "What's the worst thing that could happen if we did do this?" And then think it through before making any hard and fast decisions.

Dozens of studies show that social information plays a vital role in decision-making—especially when risk is involved. And those studies suggest that the ventromedial prefrontal cortex (VMPFC), our old friend the risk calculator, considers social influence a key variable in its determination of subjective value, or whether a risk is worth taking. Patients with frontotemporal lobar degeneration, a condition that results in damage to the VMPFC, make a lot of faulty decisions because they can't quite understand the importance of the social components. Studies that look at explicit social cues in decision-making, such as having another person give you advice as you are making choices, show activation of areas like the anterior cingulate cortex, which helps us to associate rewards and actions so that we can learn from past experience. What you see, time and time again, is that the meso-cortical limbic circuit puts a lot of stock in our social connections. And these connections have the power to influence whether we hit the gas or pump the brakes.

FAMILY-THINK

....

Even Kaufmann, as unconventional as she is, it not immune to group influence. And this becomes clear when you learn that she waited to write her op-ed until her husband left command and moved to a new duty station.

"My biggest concern in writing that op-ed was in terms of what might happen to my husband. It's one thing for me to speak my mind, but it's another for it to negatively impact his career," she says. "And I know that I never would have written it, I never would have been able to be completely honest in the way I needed to be honest, while he was still in command of a battalion. I couldn't risk that shit raining down on him."

Family may be one of the most important groups to consider when taking a risk. It's no wonder—the people you are closest to also suffer when you make a bad call on a risky decision. They, too, have to live with the consequences. Kaufmann does not have children. But I can't help thinking that if she were a mom, she would have been just as concerned about how that op-ed might have impacted her kids. I've certainly wondered if being a parent has changed the way I look at risk.

Thomas Hills, a psychologist at the University of Warwick who studies risk-taking, was also curious about whether having children might influence a risk-taking task. He and his colleague Dominic Fischer recruited 80 individuals to play the Balloon Analog Risk Task (BART), which, as you may recall, involves pumping up a virtual balloon; each pump nets participants a monetary reward, but if you pump too many times, the balloon goes *pop!*—and any and all monies you've earned disappear. The trick is to maximize your number of pumps and then to cash out before bursting your balloon. And speaking as someone who tends to pump more than the average person on this task, it's something that can get you feeling quite competitive quite quickly.

Hills and Fischer added a little twist to the traditional BART game, however: A photo of a man, a woman, or a baby was displayed on the screen along with the balloon. Participants were instructed to imagine that they were to share their winnings with the person in the picture.

Hills and Fischer found that men, when looking at the photos of other men, increased their risk-taking behaviors. They pumped significantly more when being gazed upon by another dude in the photograph. This, Hills says, supports an old evolutionary hypothesis called the parental investment theory.

Females have a limited number of eggs. It pays for them to be choosy about selecting a mate. They have a significant commitment, both through pregnancy and beyond, to their offspring. Males, however, are practically drowning in sperm. They can, like the proverbial honeybee, flit flower to flower, spreading their seed. Provided, of course, they can find some receptive flowers. So, the onus is on young men to convince as many of those choosy females to procreate with them. How might they do that? By engaging in attention-garnering displays and risky behavior. From beautifully feathered peacocks to perfectly gelled metrosexuals, boys have to go above and beyond to get noticed if they hope to find a good mate. And the fact that men showed this increase in risk-taking behavior on the BART, Hills argues, suggests their biology was pushing them to try to show up even an imaginary rival who might get in the way of their particular brand of parental investment.

Women, however, acted a bit differently. Overall, they tended to pump fewer times per trial than the men. But they were even more likely to hold back on the pumps when the photo of a baby was present. Photos of children appeared to make women much more risk-averse. This, too, fits with evolutionary arguments about parental investment.

"Children are something that should be protected. So it's an advantage for women to be more risk-averse when they are around children," Hills explains.

Perhaps this explains why my own risk-taking behaviors have changed since I had my son: I'd like to protect him from the consequences of my bad decisions. As I talk to Hills, I realize that the women in this particular study weren't looking at photos of their own offspring. They pumped less even in the presence of some random, unknown baby. Would the effect be stronger if participants were staring into the eyes of their own child? I have to ask.

"It's hard to imagine how it could be otherwise," Hills replies.

"What about men and their own babies? Studies have shown that having babies makes a man's testosterone level drop. Since testosterone has been linked to risk-taking, might you see more risk-aversion if men were looking at pictures of their own babies?" I ask.

"I think so. And there's some work to suggest that, when it comes to your own children, men can become more risk-averse too," he says.

POTENTIAL-MATE-THINK

Hills hypothesizes that men took more risks on the BART to dissuade potential rivals. But what about taking risks for the sole purpose of attracting a mate? There's no point in running off all those other boys in the vicinity if the female in question wouldn't have you even if you were, literally, the last man standing.

Over the past decade, myriad studies have suggested that merely being around attractive members of the opposite sex has the power to disrupt cognitive functioning—particularly for men. Put a good-looking woman in the room and Robin Williams's old adage about the big head, the little head, and only enough blood to run one or the other feels very true. But, as it turns out, the presence of attractive women does more than just get in the way of things like working memory and object recognition. It also increases risk-taking behavior. And one way it may do so is through increased testosterone.

To study this phenomenon, Richard Ronay and William von Hippel, psychologists at Australia's University of Queensland, headed to their local skate park in Brisbane. If you frequent such spots, you know that some of the stuff these kids do on their skateboards is not for the faint of heart—you'll see folks freestyling up and down half-pipes as well as sliding down railings and other structures. You'll also see them fall. A lot. And bleed and break bones and hit their heads and crash into each other, often laughing all the way. Because, even when there's no one to impress, the tricks these skaters are trying to master are fairly dangerous. So, what happens when you throw an attractive female into the mix? Might male skateboarders turn it up a notch or two? It would appear so.

Ronay and von Hippel recruited 96 male skateboarders and asked them to perform one easy trick, something they had mastered, and then one difficult trick that they could manage only approximately 50 percent of the time. In the first block of the experiment, all the participants were asked to do these tricks, 10 times each, while a male experimenter videotaped them. Easy enough, right? But in a second block, they were asked to do their tricks again—but this time, half the participants were recorded by an attractive female. At the end of the experiment, the researchers collected some saliva from each skateboarder to assess testosterone levels.

As expected, skateboarders took greater risks on their difficult tricks when they were being watched by an attractive female—leading to fewer aborted attempts. Given that the skaters were trying harder for the hot chick, the researchers saw a mix of failure and success. That is, with fewer aborted tricks, the skaters both crashed and burned more frequently but also successfully completed the trick more often than those who were being taped by the dude. Also as predicted, testosterone levels went way up when the hot female experimenter was around. Ronay and von Hippel argue that the increased risk-taking is due, at least in part, to those increased testosterone levels. As you may recall, elevated testosterone has been linked to increased risk-taking in financial markets and other domains. It would seem that it helps up the ante at the skate park too.

The authors hypothesize that having an attractive female around lessens the calculating capability of the VMPFC, the prefrontal cortex's calculator—all that testosterone means that these young men have a harder time calculating the odds and pumping the brakes. It decreases overall executive control of behavior and leads to more risky moves. But those bigger risks seem to have an evolutionary purpose, Ronay and von Hippel argue: They help young men attract good mates. Thomas Hills, the University of Warwick psychologist, agrees that it makes sense.

"From an evolutionary perspective, males need to care about getting access to females. And so, the idea is that males, when competing with one another for females, will take more risks," he says. "In our evolutionary history, it was probably rarely one-female-per-male. Assuming that's true, this starts to become a winner-take-all kind of situation. Unless the male stands out in some way, he may fail to mate entirely."

So you can see how risk-taking could be a boon in this kind of situation. Risk-taking can help a young man stand out from the crowd and get the attention of a desirable female. Risk-taking can also serve to intimidate the other young men around him, giving those potential rivals a signal to step off, the lady in question is spoken for. And so, Ronay and von Hippel argue, males may have evolved unique hormonal mechanisms to facilitate greater risk-taking around attractive females—a particular biological heritage that helps them find mates and spread all that ever loving sperm around. And doing so helps them break more than their fair share of ankles at the skate park.

THE RISKS THAT BIND US

....

This all goes to show that our social connections play a critical role in our perception and pursuit of risk. Friends, family, and co-workers still give us a lot of support—and emotional and cognitive stability. Our social groups help provide a context that determines how much risk we are willing to undertake. Even people we don't know (but may want to know) have the power to change the risk-taking calculation. And knowing that our peers have such power over what direction we take, we may be wise to take a step back and ask ourselves whether it's the right choice. Having the right team around you, at work and at home, can help you (and your meso-cortical limbic circuit) weigh all the variables in a risk calculation appropriately—and come to a sound decision.

Kaufmann believes that she has found a group of kindred spirits at the Code of Support Foundation who share a common vision and goals. And she's grateful that she's in a position where she can work directly with government agencies to help military families. But, she admits, being part of that group has made it harder for her, at times, to take a big stand on unpopular issues. She's worried about rocking the boat too much—and it potentially blowing back on Code of Support as an organization.

"Sometimes, when I'm in a meeting with someone really high-ranking, it is harder for me to speak up now. Before, I would just spring up and say what I thought. Because that was the only avenue I had to let people know about what was going on. Now I find that I have to sometimes force myself to do it," she says. "I have to really weigh the risk. Because there's a fine line between getting your voice heard and keeping your seat at the table so your organization can be seen as solution-oriented, a partner, if you will, and keep those important connections with other organizations so you can hopefully make things happen."

Even nonconformists can find themselves swayed by a group—or a baby, or romantic rival, or hot chick, for that matter. And because social influence is so powerful, Murray-Webster advocates for self-awareness when it comes to vetting any risk. She says you need to take a step back and make sure your social groups are helping you focus on the right elements of a risky decision—not redirecting your attention to variables that will ultimately lead you astray.

"It pays to take a look around and understand what is driving your attitude in a given situation. Because it's not always obvious just how much you are being influenced by others," she says. "Think about what's happening, who is involved, and who is really invested in a certain outcome. And then challenge yourself. Ask questions. You'll find that, in doing so, you'll have a better grasp on when you should take a risk and when you shouldn't."

Chapter Nine

RISK AND EMOTION

THE FIRST THING MOST PEOPLE NOTICE about John Danner is his smile. It's wide, authentic, and almost too good to be true. It's scored permanent crags and valleys into his face over his 40-odd years. So deep, perhaps, that he may have actually lost the ability to *stop* smiling at some point. Sitting down with Danner and his megawatt grin may make you think you've just met a kindergarten teacher or, perhaps, a *Sesame Street* cast member. He definitely doesn't give off the kind of vibe that would make you take him for a successful serial entrepreneur—or the kind of risk-taker that causes even Silicon Valley elites to shake their heads in wonder. He just seems too happy, too exuberant—not the kind of serious number-crunching, business-analyzing, pinstripe-wearing, moneymaking success you usually see profiled in the major business magazines.

But a successful (and risky) entrepreneur is exactly what Danner is. In fact, he's a bit of a Palo Alto, California, legend. More than two decades ago, Danner predicted the importance of advertising revenue to the World Wide Web. He was one of the first to suggest that online advertising would help pay for much of the Internet's rapidly expanding content—keeping the Web open and free to users. His first company, NetGravity, created ad servers and related tools to manage Internet advertising. When he sold the company in 2000, he could have tried to get on board with the newest tech trend, either by investing in new companies or leveraging his experience to keep up with the Internet advertising space. Instead, he took an interesting gamble: He decided he wanted to improve public education through technology. And he wanted to do it in a rather contrary and risky way.

"So many states are trying to cut off funding for schools. Every time you turn around, there's something stupid going on that makes it harder and harder to serve kids and make sure they get the education they deserve," he tells me. "It shouldn't be that way. It's wrong."

Danner wanted to found an education technology company that could serve children despite all those cuts by using online tools to fill in the gaps. But he knew he needed to do his homework first. So he went to graduate school to get his master's in education. When he finished, he taught fifth and then second grade for a couple of years. And after all that in-the-trenches kind of research, he cofounded a rather unconventional start-up called Rocketship Education.

"Rocketship has a very interesting model. Part of our day is online, part of our day is in the classroom," he says. "We have higher class sizes. We are doing whatever we can to make the model work so it is efficient and high-performing."

More computer time, bigger class sizes—these are ideas that fly in the face of what most educators advocate for in the public education system. In fact, they are ideas that fall squarely in the "what not to do" category of education ideals. Despite this, Rocketship's model is somehow getting the job done. Over the past few years, the company has shown overwhelming improvements at a number of underprivileged (not to mention underfunded) charter schools across the state of California. Contrary and risky, in this case, appear to be getting the job done.

When I ask Danner why he thinks he's been so successful—especially since, according to many education experts, Rocketship is doing all the wrong things—he brings out that smile again. "I think being a contrarian is super-important. Just looking at friends who have been successful, it would seem that if you aren't a contrarian, your chance of being unique in any space is pretty low," he says thoughtfully.

I don't feel the need to mention that contrarians are also usually seen as risk-takers. Yet, while his peers happily out him as such, Danner does not agree with that assessment. In fact, he argues that most social entrepreneurs, or entrepreneurs that build businesses with the aim of affecting social change, would not cotton to being called so either.

"A few years ago, someone wrote a book to try to figure out what makes social entrepreneurs tick," he says. "The author came to this great conclusion in talking to all these social entrepreneurs. They had almost a compulsion to do what they were doing. They felt like they had to do it. They didn't look at what they were doing as risk, because they felt so strongly that it had to be done. And if you feel like you have to do it, who cares if it's risky? You see a social problem. It has to be fixed. And so you do whatever you need to do to fix it."

John Danner approaches his life with some serious intention— as well as that big ol' smile. He sees a need—no, he *feels* a need—and is compelled to work hard and meet it. He is a man who is buoyed not only by his work but also by emotion. And, sure enough, he often relies on his feelings when it comes to figuring out whether it's worth taking a risk in his business ventures.

EMOTION VERSUS AFFECT

Bloomberg, a leading global business company, estimates that eight out of ten start-up companies will fail. Yet, despite that rather depressing statistic, Silicon Valley is full of successful serial entrepreneurs who keep trying to appropriately vet risk when it comes to investing their time and money in new ventures. The old neuroeconomic model of decision-making would say that emotions have no place in those kinds of decisions. In fact, proponents of that model might agree with *Dune* author Frank Herbert that fear—or any emotion, for that matter—is the "mind killer" and will only get in the way of success. After all, whether you just broke up with your significant other or let yourself get too excited about an unexpected round of angel funding, feelings can get in the way of optimal decisions. In the flurry of all that emotion, you might get distracted. You might inflate the importance of some variables and ignore the impact of others. And, ultimately, if you are too emotional, your poor prefrontal cortex, home to the brain's risk regulator and calculator, might miscalculate the probabilities of possible outcomes and choose unwisely. Most of us, at one time or another, have made some bad decisions when we were too emotional and have paid the price. And, thanks to all those bad decisions, psychologists and neuroscientists have gotten more interested in how the brain deals with uncertainty when we're emotional. One of those psychologists is Paul Slovic, director of the nonprofit Decision Research, which studies risky decision-making in modern life.

"Many of us who study the psychology of risk originally approached it the same way economists were thinking about it," Slovic says. "And economists were very much 'slow thinking' advocates. They thought everyone was making rather complex calculations about expected value and expected utility when it came time to make a decision. And it took us a while to come to the realization that there was this other way of thinking—something faster and, at times, much more dominant. It may not seem obvious but it is important to appreciate the subtle power of affect and feeling on our decisions. It has the power to influence our decisions in ways we're not always aware of."

Indeed, today's scientists have learned that a little emotion, or the more muted feeling of affect, isn't always such a bad thing. It's certainly not a decision killer by any means. In fact, affect can also help us better assess risk in some situations.

So what is the difference between emotion and affect? Slovic will tell you the key difference is one of magnitude. Emotions are powerful, overwhelming even. They have an evolutionary purpose: They arouse the nervous system so that we are prepared to deal with whatever the world throws at us. Emotions result in physiological changes to the body—which, in turn, influence our behavior. Think of fear. The amygdala, the brain's burglar alarm, sets off a series of signals that result in a physical, bodily response. Your heart races, your breathing rate increases, and you start to sweat. Your facial expression changes. And your body is now tensed up and ready to deal with a threat.

"Emotions are very powerful. They kind of churn us up and get us going," says Slovic. "They function to protect us from things that might harm us. But they are very stressful and take a lot out of us."

That they do. And reacting with the whole physiological punch of emotion—be it fear, anger, disgust, surprise, happiness, or sadness—every time a decision calls for emotional input would be an expensive physiological proposition. Too expensive, most likely, to keep the body going day to day. Antonio Damasio, a pioneering neuroscientist at the University of Southern California who has been studying the role of emotion on decision-making for decades, has suggested that, over time, humans evolved the ability to get the punch of emotion without having to deal with all the corresponding physiological mess. Over time, we learn from our past emotional experiences so we can call up some affect, or the essence of the emotion, to inform our decisions without elevating the heart rate and sweating through our shirt every time. This makes the decision-making process much more efficient, both physiologically and cognitively. (Not to mention, cuts down on the laundry.)

"As we make decisions, we can think about things that scare us and get the negative gist of it. That's what I call 'affect,'" says Slovic. "'Affect,' as I define it, is a feeling. Sometimes it's unconscious. But it's generally a valenced kind of feeling that what you are experiencing, or are about to experience, is good or bad. Affective feelings aren't full-blown emotions, as such, but, rather, faint whispers of emotion that guide you."

Affect is a critical part of the fast-thinking system. It is a decision-making shortcut that can help us react quickly—and, with luck, in our own best interest—as well as motivate us to do what we need to do to handle whatever is coming our way. And affect plays an important role in responding to risk. Chances are, you've felt your own faint whispers when it comes time for you to make a risky decision. It's that little voice in the back of your head telling you that you are about to do something amazingly epic—or monumentally stupid. So, how is affect changing up the risk equation? According to Damasio, it's by providing something called somatic markers, or emotional inputs that help guide the decision-making process.

SOMATIC MARKERS AND RISK

In the mid-1990s, Damasio worked with a group of patients who had brain damage to the ventromedial prefrontal cortex (VMPFC), the brain's risk calculator. If you met one of these individuals on the street, you wouldn't necessarily know that he or she had suffered such brain damage. They tend to demonstrate largely normal intelligence and problem-solving skills. But Damasio noticed something interesting about these individuals in the lab. They tended to make risky decisions in gambling tasks—and what's more, they didn't seem to learn from previous experience, but rather kept making the same high-caliber mistakes on these tests over and over again. And these deficits went far beyond lab tests. Their risky choices often led to grave financial and social losses in real life too.

It might have been easy to attribute this particular decision-making quirk to some kind of problem with attention or memory. But Damasio noted another interesting quality about these patients. They weren't all that emotive. In fact, they presented themselves with quite a flat affect—and they didn't respond to emotional situations in the same ways individuals without VMPFC damage do. This led Damasio to suggest that the real impairment here was one of emotion. Simply stated, patients with VMPFC damage were unable to use their feelings to help them make decisions. And that lack of affect, especially in situations of uncertainty, led these individuals to take more risks—as well as make less advantageous choices.

Damasio calls this theory the somatic marker hypothesis. Somatic markers are those faint whispers of emotion Slovic talked about, the associations between the situation we're encountering in the world and a corresponding emotional state. Somatic, in biological terms, relates to the body, or, more specifically, to the parts of the nervous system involved with voluntary movements or decisions. So, a somatic marker is simply a variable in the risk calculation, a small emotional indicator, or that little bit of affect, created from your experience with past outcomes that helps push you toward one decision or another.

The crux of the somatic marker theory is that emotions are essential to making good decisions, particularly decisions under risk, because they can help us assess the value of the available choices. Those markers highlight the emotional impact of the potential consequences of a decision and, in doing so, help direct our attention toward the choices that will lead, all else being equal, to more optimal outcomes.

If you recall from our previous discussions, the VMPFC, the brain's risk calculator, plays a critical role in helping to determine subjective value as we assess risk. This is the very brain area that was damaged in Damasio's poor-decision-making patients. But individuals with brain damage to the amygdala, the limbic system's burglar alarm, also have difficulty making the same kinds of decisions folks with VMPFC damage do. In both cases, it would seem, these patients are simply unable to anticipate the emotional impact of their choices—or, alternately, unable to process somatic markers, those faint wisps of emotion associated with the outcomes of past choices—when calculating the risks involved with a decision.

The sum of Damasio's research, pursued with colleague Antoine Bechara, argues that making good decisions requires both cognitive skill as well as emotional input. It's especially important when you have complicated (and conflicting) alternatives. Based on their decades of research, they argue that the amygdala, always in tune with those oh-so-important four *F*'s (fight, flight, feeding, and "reproduction"), creates affective representations, or feelings, about the rewards and punishments we encounter as we move through life. The insula, the brain area involved with so-called gut feelings, takes those representations and associates them with past experience. Or, to put it another way, the amygdala, the brain's burglar alarm, gives us those strong, visceral feelings about different situations we encounter in the world. The insula tones down those feelings a bit so we can get the gist of them, understand them in context, and then apply them to the situation at hand. When it comes time to make a decision, the VMPFC, the brain's calculator, accesses those feelings and their associations, reenacting, so to speak, the potential emotional consequences of your different choices. And it can do so both consciously, like those warning bells you sometimes hear in your head before you make a decision, and unconsciously—biasing you toward a particular outcome without your even being aware of it.

For example, let's say you have an important business development meeting on Friday morning—but you've just been invited to go to see your favorite band play live on Thursday night. How will you spend your Thursday evening? Somatic markers may guide your choice. If your promotion depends on getting this deal done, you might have a somatic marker that makes you feel anxious or sad when you consider not preparing and losing credibility in front of your colleagues. The somatic markers are telling you to stay home, practice your presentation, and get a good night's sleep. Of course, you'll probably also have a somatic marker representing how happy this particular group of musicians makes you feel when you are out dancing along with the crowd. In theory, whichever one of those two markers creates a stronger visceral reaction should win out in the end—or at least help you adapt and figure out some alternative where you can adequately prepare *and* hit the concert hall.

"Feelings can both influence us to take more risks or take less risks, depending on the nature of the scenario," says Slovic. "They are a very sophisticated compass. Feelings are tools, built through our direct experience with the world, to help us figure out which choices are good for us and bad for us. And provided our feelings are properly attuned to the world around us, to our goals and what is really important to us, what we've been told is immoral or problematic, et cetera, they are going to do a pretty good job of helping us make good decisions."

Feelings can be a great decision-making heuristic, or shortcut. Those somatic markers can lessen the burden of all that higher risk analysis and help guide you to a quick, efficient decision. But quick decisions don't always work in our favor. So are our feelings always helping us make smarter decisions—or might they also have the potential to get in our way?

THE GOOD, THE BAD, AND THE BIASED

The neuroeconomists would have you think that we decide whether or not we're going to take a risk by thoroughly analyzing it. As Harvard neuroscientist Joshua Buckholtz told us, risk is all about computing subjective value, or our assessment of the costs and benefits of each potential outcome—and what they may be worth to us personally. But, if we think about some of the big decisions we've made over the years, it becomes pretty obvious that we don't just judge a risk by thinking about it. How we feel about the situation—and the potential outcomes—also plays a critical role. Slovic argues that we have two pathways to perceive and act upon risk: risk as feelings, our gut response to danger or uncertainty; and risk as analysis, the more logical, reasoned approach. And while both are important, our feelings appear to automatically handle more of our day-to-day risk assessments. Our gut feelings, for the most part, rule.

As Slovic says, when those more subtle feelings are in tune with reality, they serve us well. But when they're not so in tune— or they end up coming on stronger than those faint whispers—we can get into trouble. If we look to common wisdom, we know that feelings are important to making good decisions. After all, how many times have you been told to "trust your gut," as you deliberated on an important life decision? I have to tell you, that's all I've been hearing from friends when I've told them about my boyfriend's unexpected marriage proposal. The answer lies within! But we also know that our gut feelings have tremendous ability to lead us astray—hence, Rob Fleming's famous line from Nick Hornby's novel *High Fidelity:* "I've been thinking with my guts since I was fourteen years old, and frankly speaking, between you and me, I have come to the conclusion that my guts have shit for brains."

Hornby makes a strong point. Emotions can often do as much harm as good when it comes to dealing with risky scenarios. And scientists are learning that emotions do so by skewing the variable weights in our risk equations.

Researchers have learned that decision outcomes that are affect-rich, or that come with significant emotional consequences, tend to skew that way. Affect-rich choices are those that are easily and vividly imagined—that produce more of a visceral and compelling reaction. And they can often amp up our gut feelings to a point where they interfere with decision-making.

Think about what happens when the national lottery tops $300 million. Like most of the general public, I stupidly run out and buy a ticket (or 20). I know that the odds of winning the Powerball grand prize are 1 in 175,223,510—I can even look it up on the lottery website. I also know that 1 in 175,223,510 are really, really shoddy odds. I am apparently more likely to be killed by an asteroid or a comet (1 in 250,000 odds there), for goodness' sake. But the idea of winning, just the happiness that colors the possibility of driving a Ferrari and traveling the globe full-time, has me spending my hard-earned money on a ticket. So, in effect, I'm risking $2 on a good feeling and a future possibility, rather than something real and tangible that would make me happy in the here and now, like a scrumptious red velvet cupcake or a catchy song from the iTunes store.

Affect-rich rewards skew the way we consider probabilities—even when we know better. For example, what would you rather have: a guaranteed $50 in cash right now or the opportunity to meet and kiss your favorite movie star? Or what about something a little more uncertain: the choice between one lottery that might net you $50 and another that puts you in the running for that kiss?

Yuval Rottenstreich and Christopher Hsee, psychologists at the University of Chicago's Center for Decision Research, used those exact questions in an experiment. The pair recruited 40 students from Rice University and gave half the certain scenario: the certain $50 or a chance at that movie star kiss, and asked them to state their preference. The other half were given the uncertain scenario: the money or the kiss lottery, and asked to make a decision.

The researchers found a significant interaction between the certain and uncertain conditions. When the cash was guaranteed, the majority of people took the money and ran. No big surprise there. You had a guaranteed outcome of real cash in hand, as opposed to some theoretical kiss. But when it was a choice between the lotteries, most people preferred a chance at swapping spit with their fantasy date. This, Rottenstreich and Hsee argue, is because the possibility of that kiss is full of affect—it can give you all those warm, tingly feelings inside. And the cash? Well, as my one friend put it, $50 doesn't even pay the electric bill. It simply doesn't have the same kind of emotional pull.

What might happen if you manipulated the affect on an equally valued prize? That was the next step for Rottenstreich and Hsee. In a second experiment, they recruited 138 undergraduates from the University of Chicago. This time, however, the lottery involved a $500 coupon that could be used toward either a once-in-a-lifetime trip to Europe or the participant's tuition costs. In this experiment students were asked how much they would be willing to pay for either a 1 percent chance or a 99 percent chance at winning both coupons. Once again, the students let their emotions guide them—they wanted in on the exciting trip, not the more practical school rebate. With a 1 percent chance lottery, participants were willing to pay a median value of $20 for a chance at Europe but only $5 for the possibility of the tuition rebate.

But something interesting happened when the researchers changed to 99 percent. With that change in odds, the participants were now willing to pay more for a shot at the tuition coupon they supposedly didn't care all that much about. It's a weird (and kind of crazy) result. Why would someone be willing to pay more for the coupon they weren't as keen on? But that's the point. The findings, the authors argued, show the emotional bias in decision-making. Affect-rich outcomes make you overestimate low probabilities and underestimate high ones—seriously biasing your decision-making ability. Here, affect gets in the way of being able to keep the numbers straight.

Is this bias present only in positive situations? What might happen if we are talking about negative outcomes? Rottenstreich and Hsee wondered that too. So, they asked a group of 156 University of Chicago undergraduates to imagine making a choice between a $20 penalty, meaning they would have to give the researchers 20 bones from their own pocket, or an electric shock. Which of the two produces a more visceral reaction in you? Having just gotten zinged by my toaster earlier this week, I'd happily hand over the $20 to avoid it again. And the study participants felt the same way. People would pay, on average, $7 to avoid the shock and only $1 to avoid the loss of $20, when the probability was at 1 percent. But again, when the lottery odds changed to 99 percent, the opposite effect happened. Folks were now willing to pay $10 to avoid the shock and $18 to avoid the loss of money. Funny how that works, no? Once again, affect got in the way of being able to appropriately calculate the odds.

Negative or positive, if the outcomes of a risky decision you envision come with a lot of emotional baggage, they have the potential to skew the way you calculate all your risk variables—and not always to your benefit. With high uncertainty, you overestimate the odds. With low, you underestimate them. The idea is that emotion, particularly intense emotion, makes you favor qualitative and positive variables. You start working with the gist instead of the actual outcome probabilities. My lottery jones—heck, America's lottery jones—is making so much more sense now. With all that giddiness about a potential win, my risk-processing center is not telling me that I have a 1 in 175,223,510 chance of winning. Instead, it's telling me I have *some* chance of winning. And the mere potential of that win—and my new Ferrari 458 Italia with heated leather seats—is absolutely thrilling. And that can make all the difference in whether you decide to buy a ticket or not.

REGULATORS, MOUNT UP!

It's clear that feelings have a lot of power when it comes to both perceiving and approaching risk. But there is a threshold. Too little emotion and you probably won't have the motivation to do much of anything. Too much emotion and you'll find yourself with a skewed—and probably detrimental—risk calculation. So, how can you make sure you are using feelings to your benefit instead of letting them get in the way of good decision-making? Mauricio Delgado, a neuroscientist who studies risk and decision-making at Rutgers University, says one thing successful risk-takers have in common is the ability to self-regulate their emotions. They find ways to allow their slow-thinking, analytical systems to come in and take a bit of the bite out of those affect-rich outcomes.

"It doesn't take all that much, actually. If you really emphasize a decision, and get emotional about it, you might not think about the risks in the right way because you are so focused on that one decision. If you take a step back, de-emphasize that one decision, put it in the context of a larger goal maybe, you are in a better position to understand what the real risks are," Delgado tells me.

How might you de-emphasize a decision? Well, there are a lot of ways to do it. Mindfulness, meditation, deliberate practice, and visualization techniques come to mind. Certainly most of the successful risk-takers I've spoken with use such methodologies to help them focus on the task at hand—as well as the big picture. But counting to ten before responding in anger, trying to rationalize your choice out loud to a friend, or even making a pro-and-con list are also decent emotional regulation methods. These are only a few of the cognitive strategies one might use to engage the slow-thinking system to bring some balance to the faster emotional one. The trick seems to be finding a way to take a moment to put everything in perspective. But Delgado wondered, would the use of such techniques end up increasing or decreasing risk-taking?

And how would their use change the way the brain's decision-making circuitry is working when we're feeling emotional?

To figure it out, Delgado scanned the brains of 30 Rutgers students as they played a simple gambling task. They had to make a choice between a guaranteed amount of money (the safe option) or a gamble for more money (the risky option) with five different levels of probability (20 percent, 35 percent, 50 percent, 65 percent, or 80 percent). For example, one trial might have a participant deciding between a definite $2.07 or a 20 percent chance of winning $10.35, another a definite $1.50 or a 65 percent chance at $3.75. You get the idea—you need to have the ability to run the numbers even as you get aroused by winning or losing. But before making such decisions, participants were given one of three important key words to consider: "Look," "Relax," or "Excite."

If participants got the word "Look," they were to think for a few seconds about the upcoming decision and the chance to win some moola. That's it—just think about the task at hand. Simple enough. "Relax," on the other hand, was a cue to actively imagine a calming, peaceful scene. You know, maybe a nice beach, the soothing sound of waves, and an ice-cold Corona. And "Excite," as you might have guessed, told participants they should use their imagery skills to conjure up some sort of rousing event before making a choice between the sure thing and the gamble—a let's-get-ready-to-rumble kind of moment. Do you think these different cues, and the corresponding emotional changes, resulted in different choices or brain activation patterns?

If you guessed yes, you're right on the money. When individuals were instructed to imagine something calm, they chose the risky option, the gamble, much less often than when they were told to think about the task at hand. That one little cue helped them to take a step back, dampen down any emotions, and make the safer choice despite the excitement of the game. And those who self-reported that they were able to successfully visualize that serene and tranquil scene—your more effective emotional regulators, if you will—chose the guaranteed money much more often than that. This, Delgado argues, demonstrates that productive use of emotional regulation strategies can mitigate risky decision-making.

When Delgado and colleagues looked at the neuroimaging results, they found that employing the "Relax" regulation technique also changed the way the brain processed risk. They had hypothesized that they would see changes to the ventral striatum, part of the basal ganglia, and that emotional regulation might have the power to change how the brain both valued the monetary reward and perceived the actual risk. And sure enough, that's exactly what they saw. When participants "relaxed" before choosing, they showed less activation in the left ventral striatum than when they just "looked." Somehow, using an emotional regulation technique helped the study participants feel less inspired by the possibility of one big reward during a single trial, calculate out the risks over the course of the whole game, and then go home with more money, since all those sure things added up across trials.

But emotional regulation doesn't change activation in just the basal ganglia, the so-called gas part of our risk-processing circuitry. The VMPFC, our prefrontal calculator, also is involved. Remember that the VMPFC encodes subjective value. And what's affect if not subjective? Scott Huettel, a neuroscientist at Duke University's

Center for Cognitive Neuroscience, noted that several neuroimaging studies investigating emotional regulation showed changes to the VMPFC, indicating that it plays an important role in cognitive control of affect. Yet he wondered if there wasn't more to it.

Huettel and his colleagues had 31 study participants learn a "cognitive reappraisal" strategy. That is, when feeling an emotional response in a scenario, they were trained to try to approach it as an objective observer, with absolutely no personal relevance. This is exactly the same strategy I use when my son tells me I am the "worst mom in the entire universe, even the *Star Wars* one," and I imagine how my kid might fare in the warm (and slimy) care of Jabba the Hutt. I have to say, it does work in quelling some of that negative emotion. The study participants were then put in the fMRI scanner and shown a series of photographs—images from the International Affective Picture System (IAPS), a unique set of photos that includes positive, negative, and neutral images ranging from photos of terribly graphic car wrecks to pretty flowers in a meadow.

For each trial, one of the emotionally valenced IAPS photos came on-screen for two seconds. Then, underneath that photo, the word "Experience" or "Detach" would come on for another two seconds, telling the participants whether they were to "experience" whatever emotional reaction they were having to the photo fully or to "detach" from it by using the cognitive appraisal strategy. After the photo disappeared, they had a few-second wait before being asked to rate how positive or negative they felt.

Huettel and colleagues found that using the cognitive appraisal strategy on negative images, like a gory car wreck or facial mutilation, increased brain activation in areas like the prefrontal cortex, as well

as other brain areas involved in awareness and control. In contrast, when study participants just let themselves experience the negative images and the feelings they inspired, there were no significant differences in blood flow. When it came to positive images, like cute puppies or laughing babies, the researchers also saw increased activation in the prefrontal cortex. But experiencing it fully, instead of detaching, brought on the blood flow to the amygdala and that calculator of subjective value, the ventromedial prefrontal cortex.

What does this mean, exactly? Well, Huettel might tell you that, when it comes to positive emotions, a regulation strategy reduces VMPFC activation while letting yourself fully experience the emotion amps it up. Translation? As the VMPFC comes up with the subjective value when we make our decisions, having unbridled happiness may distract us and inflate the probabilities of potential outcomes. All those good feelings get in the way of the numbers. Instead of paying attention to the fact that we have only a one in a million chance of seeing a particular outcome, all we consider is that there is *some* chance of it happening. And that change in perspective has the power to inspire us to be more impulsive in our choices. We buy those lottery tickets because we can imagine magnanimously spending all those millions. We pay too much for a cool car just because we love the way we look or feel when we drive it. We take more risks because we're just so damn ecstatic. And all those good feelings, which are just as important to our valuation of different options, can sway us in ways that aren't exactly optimal. They have a lot of power—and can lead us astray if we aren't regulating ourselves, or exercising proper slow-thinking measures, to keep them in check.

FEELINGS, NOTHING MORE THAN FEELINGS?

Despite all the smiles and talk of feelings, John Danner, our happy-go-lucky serial entrepreneur, would be the first to tell you that he's not an emotional person.

"I think most people would describe me as your typical engineer. I'm pretty quantified about things," he says. "But, personally, I think, especially when you are deciding to make big jumps, emotion is dominant. So as rational as we may be, or try to be, about what makes sense to do, in the end, you will always have your gut telling you, 'You need to do this.' "

And it would appear that a combination of Danner's more "quantified" nature and his feelings is what makes him so successful in the business world. Decision Research director Slovic says that, while affect is generally right on the money, it sometimes needs to be bailed out by the slow-thinking system. It would appear that's what is happening in Danner's case. He can modulate his emotion to make the choices that are right for him—as well as for his entrepreneurial ventures. And that's a valuable skill to have.

That combination of logic and emotion is why, Danner says, despite his passion for education and this rather contrarian company of his, he's already planning his exit from Rocketship. To hear him tell it, he was planning that exit from day one.

"When I started the company, I thought really hard about having a co-founder that would balance me out. Someone who is strong where I'm weak, that kind of thing," he says. "But the truth is, when I started talking to my co-founder, Preston, about starting

Rocketship, what I was really thinking about was, 'Is this the guy who can take over the company a few years down the road?' So, really, I was trying to find someone I knew could take over."

"Wait, you were already trying to find your replacement before you even started?" I ask with surprise.

"Yes," he says, laughing. "Over the past five years, we've been developing him to take over. And my hope is that, over the course of this next year or so, he'll be ready to be CEO."

"But why? You are so passionate about this."

"I generally feel that doing the right thing in the long term, which may mean making some risky moves in the short term, is the better way to go than to just mitigate risk all along the way. I believe that not changing is risky—if you don't adapt, you are going to die. And as organizations grow and get bigger, it's just gets harder and harder to adapt."

"So you can just leave?" I ask incredulously. "Just like that?"

"Yes. NetGravity was basically four years. Rocketship has now been about six years—and I want to be out before it gets to 1,000 employees and we lose our ability to move quickly and adapt. We're at about 300 employees now, and it's already getting harder. And you have to move. Not moving, not adapting, that's what ends up killing a company."

I admit, I am a little skeptical, given his passion (and his emotional investment), that he will actually leave his position at Rocketship. Yet, less than six months after our conversation, I see that Danner is true to his word. It's then that he passes the CEO torch to his co-founder, Preston Smith, and leaves the company to start a new educational venture, Zeal. Part of it has been his plan all along—but another part of his reason for leaving is that Rocketship uncovered a new need that Danner felt compelled to meet. His feelings were leading him elsewhere.

"In my opinion, the main academic problem Rocketship had was with personalizing learning for students. Trying to do that made an awful lot of work for the teachers," he says. "The idea with Zeal was to make it easier on teachers, so they can see a student, understand what they know and what they need to know, then assign a goal to them and then walk away. Now that we're up and running, students are completing about 12,000 lessons per day, and it's going really well."

Despite all that passion, despite that emotion, Danner knew when it was time to move on. He knew when it was time to create a new venture, a smaller and more agile company, to create new products that will help realize his hopes and dreams for education. He knew when it was time to move on and say goodbye.

It's a compelling act of emotional regulation, if ever there was one. And, as you look at the studies, it's clear that good regulation is key—and offers individuals important information about when it's time to let go and move on. For most of us, that's a skill that could use improvement. Successful risk-takers employ emotion-regulation strategies that allow them to de-emphasize one risky decision in the context of a larger goal. Once again, everything seems to come back to preparation and experience. But is that really all there is to it? Rutgers University's Delgado says yes and no.

"You can think about it a couple of ways. If you think of a successful dieter, someone who is trained to give up really rewarding food, you see really strong connections between the dorsolateral prefrontal cortex and ventromedial prefrontal cortex. That same connection is important in emotional regulation. So maybe, with training and successful examples of self-control, you strengthen that connection, and it helps you in future examples," he says, stopping to consider the matter for a moment. "But if it is something that we're really attached to emotionally, then we may be even more averse to taking a loss when it comes to that thing, even if it is the rational thing to do. We often don't want to dump that stock, as a trader might do. But if you can emotionally regulate, if you can make that reward less important in a top-down way, you are going to be better at knowing when it's time to move on and make a better decision for the long term."

It's clear: Emotion is important to making smart decisions. But emotion can't work all by its lonesome. For our guts to have more than "shit for brains," as novelist Hornby says, they need to be modulated by our slow-thinking systems. Our feelings, provided by circuits honed by experience, work best when they are informed by training and preparation. Emotions affect the way we make risky decisions, changing up how our prefrontal cortex reads inputs from other parts of the mesocortical limbic circuitry, and then using those inputs to calculate the numbers of any risk equation. And those differences can fundamentally change our behavior when faced with risk. And not always in a good way.

But, fear not, we are not doomed to be slaves to our feelings— despite their considerable sway over the decision-making process. We have the power to regulate our emotions to mitigate risks when necessary. Feelings definitely influence the brain systems involved in risk-taking—but, ultimately, we have a lot of say in how and where they do. By simply taking a step back and finding a way to detach from emotion to place risky decisions in the proper context, we can better ensure affect is working for us, instead of against us, as we go after the things we want most in life.

Chapter Ten

RISK AND STRESS

GET MARK WALTERS TALKING ABOUT his 17-year career in the Army's Special Forces and you'll hear some pretty outlandish stories. Of course, it's not always so easy to get Walters talking—he's naturally a bit on the reserved side. Yet, once this second-generation Special Forces operator, third-generation Army noncommissioned officer does open up (which, oftentimes, requires the right companion and a beer or two), prepare to be astonished. He's full of colorful stories about insertion dives, parachute jumps, jungle-village infiltrations, building demolitions, native wooing, and even roadkill dinner entrées. My favorite tale is about when, during a mock prisoner-of-war training exercise, he tried to rally his fellow faux-POWs to show up for an inspection sporting erections. As he tells it, I can easily picture a handful of naked, half-starved, and dirty men "saluting" their captors in this unexpected manner.

"It didn't work," he tells me with an audible sigh. "We hadn't eaten or slept in a while. But I still think it would have been funny."

I love hearing his stories. Each is more hilarious than the next—Walters has a gift for getting into all kinds of ridiculous scrapes (and is equally gifted at getting out of them), whether he has been deployed to some 'stan or is just hanging out in his own backyard.

But there is another common facet to his tales. They are often a bit nerve-wracking for me to listen to. It's probably because I'm the type of clueless civilian who has never rappelled from a helicopter with the sole intent of blowing up an al Qaeda safe house. They make me more than a tad anxious. His Special Forces team deals with extreme cold, heat, hunger, thirst, heights, and depths—not to mention enemy gunfire—on a regular basis. Outside the humor, one other common denominator is threaded into each story Walters tells. And that something is stress. Serious stress.

You may think of stress as a feeling. That's the way we talk about it, after all. We *feel* stress. It makes us mad or sad or sensitive or anxious. So while stress is linked to emotion, and can often influence our emotional states when we experience it, the two are not the same.

Scientifically, stress is defined as something that occurs "whenever a demand exceeds the regulatory capacity of an organism, particularly in situations that are unpredictable and uncontrollable." So, basically, stress is that extra tension you experience when you encounter a taxing situation. It can happen when you are taking a final exam in a tough class, when you are forced to engage in small talk with your ex at a family event, when your car breaks down on the way to an important meeting, or, if you lead a life more like Walters does, when you are trying to extract a hostage from some unfriendly drug runners in Colombia.

Stress is a state that affects us physically, mentally, and emotionally—and can have a significant impact on our behaviors. But no two people will experience stress in the same situations, or even in the same physiological or psychological ways. There are tremendous individual differences. And, as I listen to his tales, I have to believe that Walters and I are on two ends of the stress spectrum—because while I start to tense up just hearing him tell a funny tale that involves grilling up some raccoon roadkill for dinner, he seems somewhat oblivious to all the dangers he's faced.

In the past decade, "stress" has become a bit of a dirty word. It's something to be tempered, released, or avoided at all costs. Yet, individuals like Walters, who take on hero type professions, don't seem to experience stress the same way the rest of us do. In fact, some of them don't appear to react to stress at all. And Walters may even be at his best in stressful environments. He appears to get an absolute kick out of them. While most of us would run and hide, he actually manages to thrive as the world throws its worst at him.

Not all of us are the hero type, of course. But new research suggests that stress isn't quite the evil it has been made out to be. In fact, stress is actually a powerful motivator. Having some stress when you face a task often helps you perform better. Feeling anxious about your grade will probably encourage you to study hard for that final—and, ultimately, get a better score. Similarly, worrying about successfully completing your hostage extraction mission will inspire you to know the plan inside and out, bringing you closer to a good outcome. But too much stress can work against you— interfering with focus, emotional regulation, and good decision-making.

Which means stress also influences risk-taking. Because uncertainty, a key component of risk-taking, is something that often coincides with stress. So, when faced with risk, you want a happy medium. A little stress goes a long way when it comes to upping your cognitive game. But too much stress can result in physical, emotional, and psychological consequences that have the potential to get in the way of good decision-making—especially when risk is involved.

THE EFFECTS OF STRESS ON THE BRAIN

Stress has the power to affect us physically and psychologically—and it does so by activating two discrete pathways in the brain. The first system it triggers is called the sympathetic adrenomedullary (SAM) pathway, the stress system that helps spark the fight-or-flight response.

Think about the last time you were stressed-out. Maybe you were about to give a big presentation at work. Or maybe you found yourself cornered by a neighbor's unruly Doberman during your daily walk. You probably had an immediate and visceral reaction to the situation. When you're stressed, your heart rate increases, your blood pressure skyrockets, and you might get a severe case of the sweats. Those quick (and sometimes embarrassing) physical reactions are thanks to the cascade of neural impulses occurring along the SAM pathway. Stress immediately gets the hypothalamus, a small structure deep in the brain that connects the endocrine and nervous system, going. The hypothalamus then nudges the medulla, part of the adrenal system, into releasing neurochemicals like adrenaline (aka epinephrine) and noradrenaline (or norepinephrine). And that leads to a glut of glucose, the body's main energy source, being released into the body—as well as activation of the amygdala, the brain's burglar alarm. And with that, the body is alert and ready for action—whether it be to flee from the scene or to fight your way out of it. It works quickly so that you can react, adapt, and, hopefully, survive whatever has been thrown your way. And it doesn't stop there. SAM's downstream effects also influence key decision-making areas like the hippocampus, the brain's memory center, and the prefrontal cortex, our risk-taking brakes, later on down the line.

But that ol' SAM pathway doesn't work alone. Under stress, that initial hypothalamus activity also fires up a secondary pathway called the hypothalamus-pituitary-adrenal (HPA) axis, a circuit that connects the hypothalamus to the pituitary and adrenal glands. This pathway works a little more slowly than SAM and, about 20 minutes after a stressor, triggers the release of the glucocorticoid cortisol—usually referred to as just cortisol. Cortisol is a steroid hormone. And, as with the release of adrenaline, it also ups glucose levels in the blood. Beyond increased energy, the activation of the HPA axis causes changes to the limbic system, including the amygdala and hippocampus, as well as the prefrontal cortex—all areas that have glucocorticoid receptors. And, perhaps most important, cortisol results in increased production of dopamine in the prefrontal cortex, changing the way the mesocortical limbic circuitry functions.

It also bears mentioning that there are loops of both excitatory and inhibitory connections between the areas linked by the HPA axis. They are constantly adapting and updating as you deal with the stressor. Because, let's face it, not all stressful situations can be managed by putting up your dukes or making a run for it. If a stressful situation continues over time, you're going to need some resources to adjust and respond accordingly. And then to keep on adjusting. And maybe to adjust a little more after that. The slower-moving HPA axis is going to help you do just that.

These two stress pathways, taken together, get you primed and ready to handle whatever the world is throwing your way. And the right amount of stress, and its accompanying neural chemical release, can help you out when you're faced with a risky decision, increasing motivation as well as upping important cognitive skills like attention and working memory. It can also help you focus on the right factors when it comes time to calculate whether a risk is worth taking. That's why finding your stress happy medium is such a good thing.

But too much stress seems to have the opposite effect. Studies in animals and humans show that repeated or chronic stress results in fairly severe cognitive deficits—including deficits in memory and attention—two things that, when you think about it, are pretty necessary to appropriately vetting risk. So it's probably no surprise that scientists have noted that stress, and the neurochemicals released in response to it, often results in riskier behavior. Jens Pruessner, a neuroscientist from McGill University, wondered if looking at prefrontal activity might give us some insight into why that's so.

Pruessner and his colleagues recruited 50 university students to have their brains scanned and their cortisol levels measured after being exposed to a stressor: a somewhat excruciating exercise in mental math. Participants were given a multistep math problem, like 3 x 12 - 29—the hardest problems could contain up to four integers. They had to solve the problem in their head—and, of course, there was a time limit to make sure calculating the multistep equation would be as uncomfortable as possible. Participants then gave their answers to the problem using an old-fashioned on-screen rotary dial. As you can imagine, it's not the most efficient method of responding. They would have to click multiple buttons just to get the dial to land on the integer they wanted. Even after dealing with all that, though, they weren't done. Once they completed the math problem, the participants were given two pieces of feedback. First, whether they got the answer correct (or timed out before giving an answer). And second, a performance score that also just so happened to include how the other participants did on the task. No pressure—why wouldn't you want to know how well you were doing in relation to everyone else? And, oh, did I mention that the time limits varied, with each one based on how long you took on the previous problem? There's just all kinds of fun to go around here. As you might expect, it's a task that gets participants pretty frustrated pretty quickly—and therefore gets their stress systems going.

Pruessner and his colleagues found that cortisol levels went way up for participants. No real surprise there. It's the kind of task that makes me a bit anxious just reading about it—and I'm someone who likes math. But the researchers also observed an interesting pattern of activation in the brain during the task—or deactivation pattern, that is. The limbic system, instead of being hyped up as you might expect, actually showed decreased activation. Brain areas involved in memory and executive control showed reduced blood flow during the stressor. And the degree of deactivation in the hippocampus, the brain's memory center, was inversely correlated to cortisol release. The more cortisol went up, the more hippocampal activation went down.

What does this mean? Well, Pruessner would likely tell you that the limbic system has to lose some power for the body's natural stress responses to work their magic and help us adapt to the situation at hand. If we rely too much on past experience, we may take too much time, overthink things, and miss our chance to react (and survive). So, stress is, effectively, telling us not to pay so much attention to our memories and past experiences. To stop thinking and start doing. These results are in line with other studies that suggest stress has great influence over the learning and memory areas of the brain.

Which means it's possible, when we are trying to figure out whether to take a risk, that the limbic system is also losing some of its influence, including all that past experience and emotional salience. And, by doing so, it appears your brain is ignoring (or not properly weighting) some fairly pertinent data when it's calculating the risk equation. That makes some sense. If important parts of the risk circuitry aren't pulling their weight, our brains won't have all that rich, important experience information to help us make the best decision. When we react to stress, we may be better equipped to deal with what's right in front of us—but we may do so at the expense of our long-term goals.

HOW STRESS CHANGES THE RISK EQUATION

Decision-making, like any other cognitive process, is influenced by stress. Most risky decisions are made under some type of physical or psychological stressor. Heck, there are plenty of situations where just having to make a decision feels stressful in and of itself. For folks like stockbrokers, cops, emergency room personnel, firefighters, and Special Forces operators like Walters, the intersection of risk and stress is often part of the day-to-day job. So, given that scientists have observed changes to the prefrontal cortex and other key parts of the mesocortical limbic circuit under stress, how might that change the way we calculate whether a risk is worth taking?

Back in 1979, noted Princeton psychologist Daniel Kahneman, with colleague Amos Tversky, defined a particular bias they observed in decision-making called the "reflection effect." The duo noted that people tended to take more risks when the decision they faced involved a loss. For example, let's say you were offered the choice of a guaranteed $50 or, alternately, a gamble, with a one-in-three chance, to win $150. If you're smart, you'll take the $50 and run. But what happens when you reframe the scenario in terms of loss? Let's say that instead of gaining something, you are now faced with a decision about losing some cash. Now, you have a choice between a definite loss of $50 or a one-in-three shot at losing $150. Due to a natural bias against loss in general, most people take the riskier option in hopes of avoiding a loss altogether. Just a small change in the task—in the "framing," of the task, if you will—alters how people handle it.

Psychologists have long thought that this is one way stress changes cognition: by mucking up the natural checks and balances of the mesocortical limbic circuitry. And certainly, work by Pruessner and others supports that idea. Stress interferes with the slower, more rational prefrontal cortex, defusing its power to inhibit the more base desires represented by the basal ganglia, our reptilian brain. It can also downgrade the limbic system's activity, removing key emotional input. And with those two systems compromised, the brain has no choice but to fall back on more habitual behaviors. In doing so, decision-making biases or shortcuts become harder to ignore.

To look at whether stress altered the "frame" of a risky decision, Rutgers neuroscientist Mauricio Delgado recruited 33 university students to participate in a financial decision-making task. But prior to doing that task, he and his colleagues stressed out the students by using something called the cold pressor test. Basically, study participants had to immerse their dominant hand in almost-freezing water (4°C, to be exact) for two full minutes.

If you aren't a cold wimp, you may not think that this task would be all that stressful. Maybe you are one of these people who wear Birkenstocks in two feet of snow and think you could handle it just fine. But there's more going on here than just a little cold. You have the physical discomfort of the near-freezing water, sure. But you also have your own inner monologue pushing you to fight that discomfort for the two full minutes, since you do have the option to remove your hand earlier. So, here you have a test in which you not only have to bear the cold but also have to host an internal debate about keeping your hand submerged for the full two minutes as instructed or giving yourself a break and removing it earlier.

And, believe it or not, the combination of those two factors can really ramp up the stress.

After the cold pressor test, participants had to decide whether they'd prefer a guaranteed payout or a gamble. There were multiple trials: some gains, some losses. A loss trial might ask if you'd like a 20 percent chance of losing $3 or an 80 percent chance of losing $0.75. A gain trial, on the other hand, would force a choice between a 20 percent chance of winning $3 or an 80 percent chance of winning $0.75. Delgado and his colleagues varied the probabilities and dollar amounts across the different trials—but they had an equal number of gain and loss choices across the experiment.

Sure enough, Delgado and his team found that the stressor did its job. Cortisol levels went up. The study participants who'd had their hands submerged for the full two minutes made much riskier decisions when it came to loss choices than those who hadn't been stressed. This, Delgado argued, was consistent with the idea that stress mutes prefrontal cortex activity, as the stress hormone cortisol trips an efflux of dopamine into the system. Without the prefrontal cortex doing its normal job of governing the decision-making process, stressed people have to rely more on lower-level brain systems, particularly habits and biases, to make decisions.

"What was really interesting for me about this particular experiment was that it wasn't that risky behavior increased overall under stress, as one might predict. It depended on whether your choice was between gambles that could potentially result in a loss, where we tend to be risky, or in a gain, where we tend to be more conservative," Delgado says.

Given this kind of effect, training would really be a benefit when you are stressed. In the military, for example, soldiers endure a lot of training so that when the stress comes on, they can fall back on habitual systems and keep going. "Someone in the military goes through extensive training during stressful situations to mimic the real-world scenarios they face," says Delgado. "And with that training, when a situation may become excessively stressful, the well-trained soldier relies on more automatic, habitual behaviors, where a novice may be overcome by stress and unable to react."

Training not only helps a person focus when stress hits; it also may even reduce the overall stress itself. After all, if you've practiced and practiced how to respond in a high-stress situation, you start to learn what to expect. You start to learn what you can control and what you can't do anything about. You accumulate more information about the potential outcomes. You gain the requisite experience so that the VMPFC, the brain's calculator, and the DLPFC, the brain's regulator, can appropriately weight decision-making variables. And that knowledge reduces all those demands on your regulatory capacity, thereby, by definition, reducing stress. You learn, as Special Forces operator Walters puts it, "to deal with it and move on."

Walters puts great faith in his training—and the automatic kind of thinking that comes with it. He says that, when stress comes on, he can fall back on what he already knows. He has to—or else he could make costly mistakes.

"All the training is what makes a difference. And you make sure you stress people out in that training too. You test your limits—the limits of your equipment and the limits on techniques and the limits on yourself. That way, when something unexpected goes down, whether it's a man down or a longer swim than expected, you don't have to think about it. You can just do it," he tells me.

I can understand the importance of that kind of automaticity when he tells me about the time he was wounded by gunfire while on an assault mission.

"You were shot? Where?" I ask. I'm surprised. This story hasn't come up before.

"In the leg."

I ask the first—and perhaps the most inane—question that comes to mind after letting my imagination run its course. "What did it feel like?"

"It felt hot, mostly. But it was just a graze. It didn't break any bones or anything."

"What did you first think when you felt it hit you?"

"Do I need to apply a tourniquet?" he says immediately.

"Really?" I'd think that some kind of expletive might be the first reaction. Or a pathetic whimper. Either one.

"Yes. And the answer was no. It looked fine. So, once we were finished with the assault, I got to a position where I could put on a pressure dressing. That stopped the bleeding, and everything was OK. Like I said, it was just a grazing wound."

He sounds so calm and collected. It's not hard to imagine him being just as calm and collected in the moment, despite all the surrounding stress of dark, gunfire, and cold. When stress increases, those high-level, slow-thinking systems run by the prefrontal cortex turn off. In response, the intuition and automaticity provided by Walters's training kicked in—making all the difference. But could it really be that simple? I push a little.

"Other people might have gotten the same kind of wound and reacted differently. They might get hit and then freak out a little. They might react with an, 'I've been hit. I don't know what to do' or some kind of terrifying shriek. You know, as opposed to the more practical 'Do I need a tourniquet?' " I say. That other person, of course, being someone like me.

"That's when it all comes down to training," Walters says. "It doesn't matter what else is going on. You know what to do. I've had tons and tons of medical training, so if I'm bleeding, I just do what I can to stop bleeding. I know that's what I'm supposed to do. You do that and get back to the mission."

His account fits well with what neuroscientists have discovered: Stress pushes you to rely on habits instead of overly thinking things through. When he felt the burn of the bullet graze, Walters immediately fell back on his training. He automatically knew how to react to the situation. He assessed his triage needs, did what he needed to do to stop the bleeding, kept on moving, and helped his team meet their mission objectives.

TAKING YOUR TIME

Researchers have also looked into whether the amount of time that has passed after a stressful event affects risky decisions. The *when* may be important: Even with good training, the need to make more immediate decisions under stress may lead to poorer outcomes.

Remember that stress triggers two discrete pathways: the fast-acting SAM, with its release of epinephrine and norepinephrine; and the slower HPA axis, which lets loose a glut of cortisol. There is some evidence that the SAM pathway, with its release of norepinephrine, actually enhances decision-making under risk—while the HPA axis's cortisol seems to degrade it. To see whether *when* you decide matters, Oliver Wolf, a neuroscientist at Germany's University of Bochum, decided to compare decision-making on a dice game 5 minutes, 18 minutes, or 28 minutes after participants were socially stressed.

To rattle the participants, the researchers used the Trier Social Stress Test (TSST), which is designed to stress you out and get the cortisol flowing. During this 15-minute test, participants are hooked up to an IV and a heart monitor and then ushered into a room with three stern judges, a video camera, and an audio recorder. Upon introduction, the judges tell the participants they have five minutes to prepare an oral presentation—like something they'd do as part of a job interview. They are even given some paper and a pen to try to organize their thoughts. Once those five minutes are up, the paper and pen are taken away, and the participant is on. Each person now needs to give that presentation and to try to get some kind of social feedback from the judges, who have been trained to not react at all. If the participant stops talking before the full five minutes are up, he or she will be asked to continue. Just like that. An impassive, "Please continue." Again and again. Until the five minutes are up.

You'd think that would be enough to rattle someone. But in the experimental world, it's not. Following the presentation, TSST participants are then asked to count backward from 1,022 in increments of 13. And if they make a mistake while doing it? Well, they just have to start all over from the beginning. Honestly, I'm having a hard time thinking of a better way to spend 20-odd minutes. And this particular brand of good time results in the release of a lot of cortisol.

Once the participants were sufficiently stressed (confirmed by measuring cortisol levels), the risk-taking portion of the experiment began. Here, Wolf and his colleagues had participants play a computerized game of dice in which, simply stated, they had to guess what number a single die would land on after a roll. But they could hedge their bets. For a gamble of $1,000, they could bet on a single number. For $500, they could name two numbers and win if either came up. For $250, they got three out of six chances. And $100 got them four out of six. If the die landed on a number they selected, they won the money. If it didn't, they lost the same amount. So, as you can see, the bigger the probabilistic risk, the bigger the potential win or loss. And what monies they took home at the end of the experiment depended on their ability to make smart bets across multiple die throws.

When the researchers looked at how the three different time groups did on the gambling task, they found that time did matter. The individuals who performed the task 28 minutes after being stressed were much more likely to take big risks, betting on the single digit for a potential payout of $1,000, than the other two groups with better chances but lower potential wins. The individuals who made their bets 5 or 18 minutes after being stressed played it safer—and, ultimately, took home more money. This, Wolf argues, supports the idea that the initial release of neurotransmitters like norepinephrine from the SAM system right after being stressed can actually help you make better decisions. But once that HPA axis and its resulting cortisol kick in, the likelihood of a more ill-advised gamble goes up. When it comes to stress and risk, it appears that timing is important.

I SAY STRESS, YOU SAY NO

I've already said that not all stressors are created equal—the neurobiological consequences of one type of stressor may be different from those of another. Different situations will lead to different responses. We know that stress triggers two important pathways in the brain. We understand that once those pathways are triggered, the way we consider and act on risky decisions changes—the limbic system loses some of its power, and we fall back on habit and training. We've seen that when we have to decide can influence this process too—leading us to make bigger gambles as more time passes. But there's another important question that needs to be answered: How much stress does one need to make an optimal decision? How much stress is too much?

When I ask Mauricio Delgado, he laughs a bit. "What is enough stress, what is too much stress—well, that's going to vary quite a bit from person to person," he tells me. "For some individuals, even a little bit of stress that occurs on a daily basis—like stress elicited by deadlines—is too much. While others can't even get moving unless that stress is up to a certain level—think about those who wait until the absolute last minute to complete a deadline. It really depends on the individual."

And those individual differences are important when it comes to risky decisions. Knowing what kind of natural risk-taker you are is definitely a boon when you consider stress and risk-taking—it may help you understand whether acute or chronic stress tends to push you to go out and take more risks (or, alternately, to hide in a closet with a paper bag over your head).

For example, Delgado notes that the kind of stress a soldier faces would probably flatten a good number of us (with or without the proper training). And as I sit across from Walters at dinner, I understand that, while stress can change how we approach risk, it likely does so in a very different way in him than it does in me. I feel like we are at opposite ends of the stress seesaw. I'm not sure he's met a situation where the demand exceeds his regulatory capacity. I have to wonder if he ever will. I, however, get frustrated by little things like work deadlines and dinner prep. But when I mention how different I think we are, he shrugs. He tells me that dealing with risk is simply about good management. If you ask him, it's really just a matter of training and proper planning.

"I think maybe we accept more risk because we live in an environment where risk is constant. Maybe you become inoculated—so that what people view as risk just doesn't seem so risky anymore," he says. "I don't think I take that many risks. I truly don't."

"You jump out of airplanes! You rescue hostages! You do all kinds of things that most people would think are crazy!" I reply.

He looks a little exasperated with me. Still, he sighs and decides to enlighten me anyway.

"So, if I jump out of a plane, is that a risk? Well, there's risk in just about anything you do. There's risk if I drive down the street in my car, though most people might not see it that way," he explains. "But let's think it through. If I jump out of a plane without a parachute, then, obviously, there is very, very high risk. That's not smart. I'm probably going to die. If I jump out with a parachute, that's a whole lot better. Less chance of death there. If I jump out of a plane with a parachute and I've been trained to do that, even better. If I jump out with a parachute and I've been trained and an experienced jumpmaster checks out my equipment before I go, and, hey, I did a jump refresher just prior to the jump to keep my training current, then I'm pretty safe. And if that airplane crew is trained with airborne ops, then it's crazy safe. I'm covered. When you take it apart, and look at all these factors that mitigate your risk, and see what's left, you get the residual risk. And that's truly the risk you are taking. And, in the case of making a jump, when you look at all the factors when I jump, there's actually very little risk involved."

He has a point. With all that training, he's not stressing about the same things I would stress about. His experience means he can look past the factors I might find stressful and consider those residual risks. I get it.

His words sound very familiar—he seems to take a similar approach to risk management as most of the other risk-takers I've spoken with. He's prepared, he's experienced, and he knows how to regulate his emotions and actions. But it's hard to ignore that Walters is a bit different. He doesn't mind the cold, the heat, the hunger, the jumps, the dives, the guns, or the hostile territory. He can handle extended stays away from family and friends. He appears to possess a natural resilience that's hard to explain. It would be all too easy to just say he was born this way and be done with it. After all, he's a second-generation Special Forces operator. The men in his family have always served—and usually in pretty risky jobs. Might it be that Walters has a particular genetic disposition that makes him more immune to stress than others? It's certainly possible.

But a disposition isn't the only factor at play here. As Walters breaks down risk for me, it's clear that he is blessed in training. When the proverbial shit hits the fan, and the brain defaults to more automatic behaviors, he has all the best kind of habits to fall back on. The kind of habits that are going to help him deal with both stress and risk in an optimal way. But, the majority of us aren't spending our working hours training for our next combat mission (or making life-or-death decisions, for that matter).

So what's the non–Special Forces type to do in the face of everyday stress? Understand how stress can influence decision-making. You can help make more optimal decisions when you understand that stress has the power to alter how you perceive risks. Recognize that stress changes the frame of a problem—and may make you focus more on potential losses than on potential gains. Understand that stress may result in more decision-making shortcuts, with slow-thinking brain systems, like the limbic system, not being able to offer as much input on your choices as it would in less stressful times. Appreciate, that all other things being equal, taking your time to think things through before making a risky decision under stress isn't always the best way to go. And, most important, if you have experience and training in a particular arena, use it! Allow that automatic thinking to take over when times get tough. Overthinking things, with all those neurochemicals coursing through your brain, may push you in the wrong direction.

Again, not all stressors are equal. Nor are individuals in how they deal with the intersection of stress and risk. And when I say as much out loud, Walters agrees. He repeats the idea that his job, with all its training and planning, just does not seem all that stressful or risky to him.

"You know what? We're the luckiest dudes on the fucking planet. We are so lucky in what we get to do in life. We scuba dive. We jump out of planes. We blow shit up. We go to foreign lands. We do great things. There is nothing better than what we do for a living," he tells me, his face breaking into a wide smile. "I would be scared to death to work at some normal job in an office. Those guys are the brave guys—the dude working behind the sporting goods counter at Walmart or some guy doing nothing but making PowerPoint presentations all day. They are the ones taking the real risks. And what they risk is leading a miserable and boring life. That's a far worse risk, in my opinion."

That's certainly something to ponder as I make my way back home—to another night clicking away at my computer screen.

Chapter Eleven

·······································

RISK AND RECOVERY

HERE IS A FUN—and likely unsurprising—fact about me: I dislike failure immensely.

It is a by-product, I'm sure, of my type A nature. I hate to fail. *Hate* it. It always ends up being a big blow to my ego, even when the failure isn't really all that big of a deal. (Honestly, should an inability to make heads or tails out of a Nutella-stuffed chocolate chip cookie recipe really define me as a cook, a mom, or a person? Probably not, yet that's the kind of place I end up going when more Nutella ends up in my hair than in the cookies.) Still, this hatred, perhaps even fear, of failure affects my decision-making process in the most obvious of ways. I often find myself hesitating, overthinking my options, and just generally stressing out when it's time to make a choice that comes with a high risk of failure. And, unfortunately, all that mental hand-wringing tends to all but guarantee an unsuccessful result.

I know this feeling isn't all that uncommon. No one likes to make mistakes, especially those of the unnecessary variety. Yet, a lot of people learn to not only tolerate failure but also appreciate it. And that's because, deep down, they know that mistakes have the potential to offer just as much opportunity for learning—perhaps even more—as success does. In fact, in all those modern-day fairy tales about risky decisions leading to big wins, getting acclimated to failure seems to be a critical part of finding success.

Think about the last profile you read about a successful celebrity, sports hero, or CEO. Somewhere, among all the talk of victories and triumphs, you'll find at least one mention of some serious woe. J. K. Rowling, single mum and aspiring author, was rejected a dozen times before *Harry Potter* was published to international acclaim. Apple may refer to the late Steve Jobs as its creative visionary—but it actually fired him before bringing him back to create all that iMagic that people love so much. Kurt Warner, the famed St. Louis Rams quarterback who walked away from Superbowl XXXIV with the Most Valuable Player award, actually spent what some might say are the most important years for a player, those few right after college, stocking shelves at a supermarket instead of throwing touchdown passes after he was cut from the Green Bay Packers. You get the idea: Most victories have some kind of serious hard-luck story lurking in the background. Somehow, someway, the most successful people seem to take disaster in stride. In fact, they seem to have an uncanny ability to recover from their screwups, both big and small, in ways that others can't. Even—no, *especially*—when a significant amount of risk is involved.

Take Dr. David Baskin, a neurosurgeon at Houston, Texas's top-rated Methodist Hospital. A jovial yet commanding 61-year-old, Baskin has been cutting open brains for nearly 30 years. He specializes in risky surgeries, particularly large and stubborn brain tumors that are nearly impossible to remove. Many of his patients find him after they've been told by other doctors that they are beyond hope—that surgical excision is all but impossible. Given his particular specialty, he knows that every time he scrubs up for a multihour surgery, there's a high likelihood that he will encounter a problem that, if not handled in precisely the right way, could result in a patient's significant injury or death.

"That's the thing about neurosurgery—there's very little we do that can't produce a catastrophic outcome if it goes wrong," he tells me. "If we operate on the spine and make a mistake, someone can be paralyzed. If we operate on the brain and make an error, the result can be a stroke or a coma. In so many of these surgeries, one false move and you can end up with not just death, but a fate worse than death. So every time we show up in the morning to do one of these operations, the risks involved have to be in the back of our minds. We have to find a way to deal with them—and it's a very fine line between putting the risks aside enough to do your job but not aside so much that you become cavalier about them."

This is a man who can take risks, and the mistakes that often accompany them, in stride. Suddenly, I feel a little ashamed—after listening to Baskin, getting frazzled about baking shenanigans seems absolutely absurd. There's a lot to be learned from recovering from your own mistakes.

To put the idea of recovery in perspective, and catch a glimpse of how an expert manages uncertainty with the highest of stakes, I head to Houston Methodist to observe Baskin remove a large meningioma, a fast-growing brain tumor that develops in the meninges, the fragile, filmy membranes that envelop the brain and spinal cord, from behind the eyes of a middle-aged female patient. The hospital and patient have kindly granted me permission to watch the surgery—and see Dr. Baskin and his team in action.

When I arrive at the operating room, Baskin greets me warmly and takes me over to view the MRI films on a light board in the back of the OR. Even from a distance of 20 feet, I can see the tumor, a staggering, solid white entity in the middle of the muted grays making up the scan of this woman's brain. As we approach the light board, I realize that the image is even more startling up close.

"This woman came into the office reporting a loss of vision. She started out just thinking her vision was a little blurry, and then, by the time she realized something was really wrong, she could barely see," he tells me, circling the tumor with his finger.

It's obvious why. The tumor, about the size of a grapefruit, is right behind her eyes, pushing the optic nerves, the cranial nerves that transmit visual information from the eye's retina to the brain, completely out of alignment. If the tumor were to remain, it would obliterate the patient's vision permanently, as well as cause a variety of cognitive problems with memory, attention, and movement— and ultimately, as it grew larger and larger, lead to her death. While other surgeons might have balked at excision because of the tumor's size and reach, Baskin carefully balances the potential risks of surgery with the possible outcomes if no intervention is performed.

"You have to think you can make a difference—and get a good outcome," he explains. "If the patient is going to be in terrible trouble and dead shortly, that gives you a little more motivation to take on something really challenging. But even knowing that,

I need to be able to see a successful outcome. I have to believe I can succeed. It's not about the risk for me. There are many, many risks involved in neurosurgery. It's about finding the path that will lead to success."

After reviewing the patient's case, Baskin believes he has found such a path. He outlines the upcoming procedure, which he estimates will take between seven and eight hours, maybe longer, depending on what roadblocks he and his team might hit along the way. Using the MRI films of the patient to help illustrate what's to come, he explains that he and a seventh-year surgical resident are going to make an incision at the crown of the head and then carefully, punctiliously peel the scalp down to the eye sockets. After drilling a series of holes into the cranium, they'll use a fine bone saw to cut the bone hole-to-hole, like a surgical connect-the-dots game, so that they can remove the skull plate and expose the brain. But, according to Baskin, that's the simple part of the surgery.

Once the cranium is open, they will have to open the brain's lining and cut the membrane spanning a major fissure that connects the frontal and temporal lobes in the cerebral cortex. And that's where it starts to get tricky. The carotid artery and its branches lie in the surgeons' path. Baskin tells me that there's a potential of nicking the artery or one of its branches at some point during the excision, because the tumor is adhered to them. That would result in a lot of bleeding. And, if unchecked, could result in the patient's having a major stroke. The tumor also has a number of large feeding arteries supplying it with blood, which almost certainly will bleed once they go in. But even if they can control the bleeding, they still have the tumor itself to contend with.

"I always say that a brain tumor is like having delicate wet noodles wrapped inside a hunk of concrete," he says, balling up his fist to represent the concrete. "The nerves are very soft and flexible, like noodles. But the tumor is quite hard and firm, like concrete. So you have to chip away at this giant tumor and try to minimize the damage to the noodles inside as you do it. It's a bit of an art form."

But Baskin isn't done explaining all the risks involved with this particular surgery. His finger moves down the MRI scan to the patient's nose. "One other thing: This tumor is so big that it has grown into the sinuses," he tells me. One false move during the excision and the lining of the brain will be violated, causing cerebrospinal fluid to leak out the nose, he explains. "That's another issue," he says, tracing his finger down the scan. "If we don't do something about that, that fluid will leak out. With such a leak left untreated, she'll develop a life-threatening meningitis. So we need to be very careful as we're working in there."

As Baskin leaves me to approach the patient and get started, I'm feeling a little anxious at all the things that could, and likely will, go wrong. He, however, seems unfazed.

THINKING AHEAD

....

How can Baskin take so many risks, with such great potential for "catastrophic events," in stride? To start, by appropriately setting expectations. Baskin's extensive training and experience—four years of medical school, seven years of residency, decades of practice, and, now, heading up a program that trains new surgeons—all comes together so that he "knows the knowns" and can think through the potential unknowns. Here's where preparation comes into play again. The good doctor goes through each of his cases with exacting detail and imagines how he is going to proceed with the surgery, step by careful step.

"I look at the films. I look at the MRI scans. I carefully consider the patient's history and physical examination. And then I think about how I'm going to approach the tumor. While doing that, I'll ask myself, 'What are the four or five things that could go wrong?' And if those things go wrong, what I am going to do about it?" he tells me. "This becomes second nature with experience, but I think that, no matter how experienced you are, you need to mentally prepare yourself for those high-risk things. Because these are high-risk surgeries. By definition, unexpected and potentially catastrophic events are going to occur. You need to be prepared to deal with them. You need to set your expectations. And you need to visualize a clear path to success."

Baskin talks about this preparation as a rehearsal—and that mental rehearsal always has him thinking ahead. "There are lots of problems that are hard to get out of. When you are facing so many possible unexpected outcomes, you need to not just think about what will happen if you encounter only one of them. Instead, you need to consider all of them. You ask yourself, what happens if an artery tears? You need to think about what kind of clip you'd use if an artery tears. And if that clip tears the artery, what kind of suture do you use? What if the suture is too small? Too big? Successfully navigating an environment with so many risks requires an ability to think three, four, five—heck, ten steps down the road."

It may not surprise you that such contingency planning is mediated by the benevolent overlord of the mesocortical limbic circuit, the prefrontal cortex. Researchers have wondered for decades how the brain handles errors—and, once they are recognized, changes the course of action in response. After all, to survive in the world, humans require a great deal of flexibility in the decision-making process. Even more so when risk or uncertainty is involved. We have to learn how to adapt if we are going to survive.

You see, unexpected outcomes result in a glut of dopamine in areas like the basal ganglia—but dopamine levels in the prefrontal cortex actually go down. That reduction in dopamine is a signal to the prefrontal cortex that it may be time to stop what it's currently doing, recalculate the risk variables, and then switch to a new, more beneficial plan of action. There's a saying that doing the same thing over and over again and expecting a different outcome is the definition of insanity. But it may actually be the result of too much dopamine in the prefrontal cortex. In fact, studies have shown that, when dopamine levels are boosted by a drug, the ability to easily switch from one action to another after noticing an error or a change in outcome probabilities is compromised—resulting in a lot more mistakes.

So, how can you avoid such costly mistakes when faced with risk? Once again, it seems to all come back to experience. Experience, gained through deliberate practice, is what helps our prefrontal cortex to mature—and to learn how to appropriately respond to the world around us. And Baskin says that surgical training programs make sure that their students get plenty of that deliberate practice. A critical part of medical training is learning about contingency plans—so residents have good alternative options when they encounter an issue or error. Teachers and mentors are constantly asking young residents, "What would you do if . . . ?" both in and out of the operating room. And that constant grilling means that thinking ahead becomes second nature—and that the prefrontal cortex is primed to deal with uncertainty and error (and not overproduce dopamine). When you have only five or ten seconds to make a decision that will profoundly affect the patient's outcome, having those abilities is crucial to risky decision-making—and making the right call when you encounter a problem.

Baskin joins the surgical team just as his resident has completed the neurosurgical equivalent of scalping. He has made a long incision across the patient's head and is now delicately peeling the skin away from the skull in a way that is reminiscent of both peeling a plum and removing the sheet of protective film from a new smartphone screen. I'm invited to stand just a few feet away—perched on a step stool so that I am out of the way yet can get a bird's-eye view of the craniotomy. And I gawp with more than a little awe as they remove the top of the patient's skull, revealing her brain for the first time.

It's funny: I've been looking to the brain this whole time to help me learn how to better manage risk in my own life. Now I see one in all its glory—pink, glistening, and waiting for surgical intervention. As Baskin gently cuts into the frontal lobe, the very part of the brain that is mediating his own ability to successfully visualize a path forward (and deal with any potential errors he may encounter along the way), I find myself a bit overcome. There are so many mysteries contained within those inimitable folds—if only we had the right tools to discover them.

THE POWER OF SMALL WINS

Part of setting expectations and visualizing a path for success are appreciating what psychologists call "small wins." Baskin visualizes his path toward success by considering the smaller subgoals he needs to meet along the way, including potential pitfalls he may encounter and how he'll manage them. He knows that any big response is the product of many smaller yet interrelated steps. By turning his focus to the small things, the things he knows he can control, he can envision how to get an optimal outcome even in such a risky situation.

What's the best way to eat an elephant? Answer: One bite at a time. And, for decades, psychologists have seen that the most successful way to reach a goal is to focus not on the end point but to celebrate the smaller, often seemingly inconsequential steps that will eventually get you there. A small win is defined as a "concrete, complete, implemented outcome of moderate importance." It's a basic tenet of the Alcoholics Anonymous "one day at a time" philosophy. Think about it. By focusing on getting through the day without a drink, the ideal of staying sober for the rest of your life doesn't seem quite as daunting. You celebrate the small wins—and that helps motivate you to work toward your larger ambitions.

How do small wins help with the big picture? It comes down to arousal—which, in terms of stress and emotion, can both help and hinder decision-making. The right amount helps up your energy, keep you motivated, and make your attention more selective. That selective attention can help you better perceive and tend to any risks you might face. That optimal level of arousal means the brain's risk-processing and decision-making systems are focused on only the most pertinent factors—so that you can fall back on your intuition and habits. And all those positive benefits of arousal work together to help you improve performance on difficult tasks. But, as anyone who has ever been overwhelmed by a task knows, too much arousal can really impair performance, getting in the way of you reaching your goals.

That's where focusing on small wins comes in. It can help keep arousal at that optimal level. And now that I see Baskin and his team in action, I understand how important each small win is to helping a multiple-hour surgery move along with confidence. Once the patient's cranium is lifted off the top of the head, Baskin notices that her brain is remarkably swollen. He checks in with the anesthesiologist to determine what drugs were used. Satisfied with the answer, he puts down his scalpel and focuses on reducing the swelling. Baskin calls for a consult—and then lowers and lifts the surgical table as he waits.

"Sometimes, just raising the head of the table a bit can help reduce the swelling and stabilize things," he says, looking back at me. And this one little thing does the trick. By the time a consulting doctor appears, the swelling has visibly diminished. Baskin thanks his colleague with a satisfied smile and gets back to work. It's a small win—especially knowing that there's still so much work ahead. But it's clear that Baskin is buoyed by it.

Small wins have the power to make you feel like you are in control—and set you up to tackle the next subgoal in your path with conviction and faith that you can get the job done. As Baskin and his team cut down into the brain of the patient, I can see the value of that kind of focus here. Brain surgery is meticulous, meticulous work. Any move has to be made with the understanding that, eventually, "Humpty Dumpty" has to be put back together again. Each small cut to this patient's brain will have to be repaired. For every step forward, the surgical team has to consider how they will step back as they close. Each small win, each step forward, preserves gains toward the final goal—and makes the entire surgery seem more manageable. And that helps to mitigate the risks involved.

Focusing on small wins also helps with perseverance in the face of a daunting task. Breaking down a bigger task into small subgoals, and then ticking those off one by one, appears to help the surgeons move forward—even as they hit the unexpected. We are now three hours into the surgery and they are standing strong. I'm only observing and my legs are starting to cramp up. Yet neither Baskin nor any other member of his team seems the least bit fatigued. They remain totally focused on the task at hand—despite several unexpected setbacks including that initial brain swelling, a broken instrument, and, now, an unexpected tear in a blood vessel as they separate the meninges. They take each problem in stride—and keep working toward the larger goal of getting to and then removing the tumor.

Baskin explains that, once the team actually reaches the tumor, they will take it out tiny piece by tiny piece. "Once we get there, bit by bit, we'll cut through the tumor, and it will be picked up by suction. We'll be doing that for a number of hours," he says. "It's very slow-going work. But, like I tell my residents, as long as you operate faster than the tumor grows, you're still going to win." He smiles widely as he delivers that clincher—and I'm once again reminded that we've already been in the OR for hours and the team hasn't even gotten to the tumor yet. Slow-going work, indeed.

THE POWER OF CONTROL

Self-control also plays a role in working toward long-term goals in the face of mistakes and adversity. Research has long shown that individuals who can look to the future and consider the long-term consequences of their decisions tend to make more optimal (and successful) choices than more impulsive types. It all goes back to living in a hospitable world. We need our neurobiological brakes—the power to say no (or, at the very least, not now)—when we are in pursuit of a reward. It can't be "me, me, me, now, now, now" all the time. We can't eat everything we want to eat, sleep with everyone we want to sleep with, and do everything we want to do in the immediate moment. It's just not good for us—or the people who have to live with us. But self-control does more than just help us remain healthy, safe, and bearable to our loved ones. Individuals with good self-control tend to better persist when they encounter barriers. Baskin is living proof of this. And it also seems that feeling *in control* of a situation is crucial to accomplishing your goals when it comes to recovering from mistakes or obstructions.

Imagine that you are a college student and only one class away from graduating with your bachelor's degree. But then, unexpectedly, you receive a letter warning that you may not be able to reach that important milestone because you failed your midterm. Now, there could be a number of reasons why you failed. But let's say one scenario is that you didn't study enough for the test—and then went out partying the night before. Between the two, you just weren't in the best test-taking shape come morning. A second scenario is one in which the professor tells the class that he designed the test to be impossible and only the top 5 percent of students will pass. Out of these two possible scenarios, which is going to inspire you to persist, work harder, and get to your goal of graduating: your own personal failure to study or the professor with the unreasonable grading curve? All else being equal, the failure to study is going to be more motivating. Because, honestly, that's the only option that you have the power to do something about. And Mauricio Delgado, the risk researcher from Rutgers, says that feeling like you have control over the outcome is a critical component as you try to achieve your goals.

"It's incredible—there is always an urge to be in control. Feeling a lack of control is very aversive," he says. "When we do experiments where we just measure how much people value control, we see the reward centers of the brain light up when they have a choice compared to when they don't have a choice, even though they get the same reward in both cases. There appears to be some inherent value to just being in control, to having the opportunity to exert your will by making a choice."

Those reward centers Delgado is speaking of are part of the basal ganglia. So it would appear that being in control helps push that proverbial gas pedal as you work toward a goal. And it makes sense. I think about the traffic I encountered on my way to the hospital the morning of the surgery. Houston is well known for its grid-lock—and, like most morning commuters, I sat, barely moving, for a good 20 minutes. And despite the fact that no lanes on the highway were making much progress, every time I saw a bit of an opening to my left or right, I'd shift lanes just to go somewhere, anywhere! And I'd do so even if that shift got me moving only a few feet. Many of my fellow drivers were doing the same. Even in a situation as uncontrollable as traffic, we embrace any action that makes us feel like we have some kind of power—even if it doesn't really help us get to our destination any faster. It's enough that it helps to motivate us to keep going, to stick it out, to keep moving forward toward our goal even when we encounter setbacks along the way.

To study this phenomenon, Delgado and company recruited 20 students to play a computerized task that measured how they responded to setbacks as they tried to reach a goal. The task was fairly simple—just using a mouse to move a stick figure down one of three paths. Each path had a number of points associated with it—and if the participants could successfully move the little stick guy on down a chosen line, they'd receive the associated points. Sounds simple enough, right? But, occasionally, randomly, there would be a roadblock. An orange or a purple triangle would show up in the path, blocking the stick figure's way. If the triangle was orange, the participant was stuck, with no way to get around it except to go back to the beginning and try again. But if it was purple, there was a one-in-four chance of removing the obstacle by pressing a key on the keyboard. So, while players would still have to go back to the beginning of the path if they chose the wrong key, they could make trial-and-error guesses until they cleared the path.

The idea here was to look at how a sense of control influenced a person's willingness to take risks. With the orange triangle, participants had no control over the outcome. They could go back to the beginning and try again—but if the orange triangle remained, they weren't going to get to the end of the path no matter what they did. With the purple triangle, however, participants had a one-in-four chance to surmount the obstacle and get to the end of the path they initially chose—which was likely the path with the most points. So, it probably doesn't surprise you that, despite the fact that both obstacles were determined by chance, and they were both equally likely to show up across the different trials, the study participants were more likely to keep trying on a high-point path when they hit a purple, or controllable, triangle than an orange, or uncontrollable, one. Those uncontrollable obstacles did not inspire persistence—and, as trials went on, participants often ended up selecting a different (and lower point value) path when that pesky orange triangle showed up. Who wants to keep trying to fix something they literally have no control over? I know, I know—it seems pretty obvious. No one wants to try to risk too much on that. No one sane, anyway.

"The idea here is that once you fail or get negative feedback as you are trying to reach a goal, you are more likely to persist with your goal when you perceive that you have control and can avoid future setbacks or negative feedback," says Delgado. "When you have control, and you know what you have to do, that negative feedback can actually drive you to persist more and to work harder to achieve your goal."

So, my fruitless traffic maneuvers were doing something to help me, even if they weren't getting me to my destination any faster. They were helping me persist in my attempt to get to the hospital in spite of all the annoying traffic—instead of just pulling into the first driveway and taking a nap. (And don't think pulling over didn't cross my mind.) So, what brain real estate might be behind this kind of persistence in the face of a rather frustrating task? Delgado and colleagues used fMRI scanning to take a look.

Previous studies have found that negative outcomes result in decreased activity in the mesocortical limbic pathway, the risk-processing circuit. As Michael Frank, the Brown University neuroscientist who studies the basal ganglia, would tell you, negative outcomes can facilitate learning as much as positive ones.

Why is this important? Dopamine influences how much risk you are willing to handle. Frank says the basal ganglia don't appear to calculate a single representation of a potential outcome that includes both the positive and negative consequences of a decision. Rather, the basal ganglia store the positive and negative values separately in two distinct pathways in the striatum, a key part of the basal ganglia that helps encode value. The amount of dopamine in the brain determines whether you pay more attention to potential rewards or potential losses as you calculate your choice.

"If dopamine levels are high, you're going to make choices mostly based on reward, almost as if you don't care or aren't representing possible losses. It's going to boost the pathway that represents the reward and you'll probably take more risks," Frank explains. "If dopamine levels are low, the opposite will happen—you'll be much more risk-averse because the representation of the potential negative outcome is now more enhanced."

For example, if you shock a rat a few times after it pulls a lever, dopamine will go down in the basal ganglia, and it'll quickly learn not only to avoid pulling the lever but also to stay far, far away from it. But if you shock the rat *and* give it some very special reward—some kind of drug or sugary treat—it'll get a mix of dopamine signals, which the prefrontal cortex, the brain's risk calculator and regulator, needs to sort out. With the right mix of dopamine signals in the brain, the rat in the shock-and-sugar scenario won't apply the brakes. Rather, it will persist and pull that lever, despite all that extra (and unwanted) electricity.

We humans aren't so different. In fact, that's exactly what Delgado and company saw when they looked at the brain during the triangle task. There was diminished activity in the ventral striatum when the participants hit the orange roadblocks. They were getting a signal to stop pursuit. But, with the controllable, purple obstacles, there was an even greater dearth of activity in the prefrontal cortex, the risk-processing brakes—which correlated nicely with the fact that participants persisted and kept trying to go down the high-value path despite the obstacle. Taken together, the potential reward plus that feeling of control proved more motivating than the risk of failure.

"What we're seeing is that when faced with a setback in a situation perceived as controllable, that negative feedback activity in the striatum correlates with behavioral change," says Delgado. "It is leading you to persist more, a sort of negative reinforcement for behavior." Simply stated, being able to go back and try again, to control the situation, counteracts that negative feedback in the basal ganglia—loosening up the brakes and pushing you to continue pursuing your goal.

I think of this study as I watch Baskin and his neurosurgery team work on the patient. A few hours into the surgery, as the surgical resident cuts slowly, meticulously down into the brain so the team can get to the tumor, he hits a blood vessel. He looks up and makes eye contact with Baskin. In response, Baskin peers into the microscope to get a better look and says, "Oh, would you look at that! She's started bleeding like crazy," he calmly tells me. "We're now going to try to find the bleeder and repair it."

Baskin nudges the resident out of the way and takes over. He changes the situation so that he is now in control—and starts searching diligently, with the help of a microscope and the eyes of the resident, cauterizing small areas around the blood vessel as he goes. Baskin told me from the beginning that this kind of bleeding was not only possible but also likely—this kind of tumor is known for attaching itself to blood vessels, warping them into odd shapes as it sucks up the nutrients it needs to grow from them.

"It's not really that much bleeding. It looks like much more under the microscope," he says. "But still, it's enough. We need to get in there and fix it." He works for a few more minutes, trying to identify the exact source of the bleed. Once he finds it, and fixes it, he looks to the team. "We need a new strategy here." He looks over at me to explain further. "This plan of attack is not working. We need a new plan of attack, and we need to change it on the fly, because of this bleeding. We don't want to deal with any more of these."

At this point, Baskin and his team could back out and close up. A damaged blood vessel is no joke—and has potential to cause problems down the line. Some might see it as a sign that it's time to stop the surgery and maybe try again another day. But, just as if Baskin were running up against a purple triangle in Delgado's study, he knows he can control this situation. He has the skills and know-how to fix the bleed. He has the experience to see alternate paths to success to get this tumor out. And he knows adjusting his behavior—his plan of attack—can make a difference. And so he persists. I'm certain that's something all Baskin's patients, especially the woman currently lying on the surgical table, appreciate about him.

THE POWER OF MISTAKES

Baskin tells me that the most successful surgeons in the world are very certain of their abilities—but they balance that confidence with a healthy fear and respect for what they do each day. "It may seem contradictory—how you can have extreme confidence but still have that fear and respect. But you actually can. But it takes a certain amount of training. You have to train yourself, when you have a job like this, to show up in the morning thinking carefully about all the issues, thinking really hard about all the things that could go wrong, but also certain that, no matter what, you're going to get through it. You mentally prepare yourself with that balance, and it almost always leads to success."

I'm struck by Baskin's line about how it "almost always leads to success." Because, unfortunately, in the world of surgery, no matter how talented the surgeon, the worst can and does occur. Failures can happen. Today, Baskin's team is hitting a variety of roadblocks as they try to remove this tumor. And as Baskin told me initially, there's always the possibility that one problem, one error, one issue, one little uncontrollable or unexpected thing will occur—and that one thing will result in the patient's death.

Baskin still remembers his first bad outcome when he was a resident in training. "I was operating on a giant aneurysm and the patient was almost comatose. He was going to die if we didn't do the surgery. As we put a clip across the aneurysm, the entire vessel just tore. The whole vessel was abnormal. There was no way to clip it, so we had to occlude the vessel, and the patient had a stroke," he says. "I remember the moment it happened. I had this horrible, sinking feeling in my throat. I was sweating and my heart rate had to be around 190. I was just like, 'Oh my God, look what happened.' I was devastated."

So devastated, in fact, that Baskin was apprehensive about doing another surgery. So his mentor made sure he was back in the OR the next morning doing a remarkably similar aneurysm case. "You have to get back on that horse. There are always things that are beyond your control. But you need to learn to deal with that," he tells me. "Because, the thing is, in every bad outcome there is valuable information that can help you avoid problems the next time around."

The sum of those experiences has helped Baskin understand when to fight on and when to stand down. "There's that famous line, 'Those who fight and run away live to fight another day.' If you get into a situation in the OR where you know that, if you go further, you're going to have trouble, there's no dishonor in stopping or backing out," he says. "In many cases, you can stage an operation. In other words, you may get to a point and say, this vessel is so tight. So you can stop, close, and let the effects of what you've done take hold. Maybe you've taken two-thirds of the tumor out, and in doing that, the swelling will go down, there will be less pressure, and you can go back in later and finish up. I'm always willing to stop if I reach a point where the risks are too high and I'm at a safe stopping point. There is no shame in stopping. There is never any shame in doing the right thing for your patient."

It may be easier said than done, but Baskin is a big believer in letting go. He tells me that he can remember every bad outcome in his nearly 30-year career—but he has learned to put those outcomes in perspective. "When you're first starting out, any bad outcome can be totally devastating," he tells me. "If you have a catastrophic event after 10,000 surgeries, however, you can think about the 9,999 other cases that went well. That's a little more reassuring."

Baskin has another cognitive tool at his disposal that allows him to better take on risky decisions: self-awareness. He can use a process called metacognition, or, to the nonscientist, "thinking about thinking." Strong metacognition allows Baskin to be aware of that possibility of failure yet not let it deter him from giving his best effort. It permits him to let go of mistakes after they happen and to learn from them so he can make better decisions the next time around. And it may not surprise you to learn that the neural seat of metacognition has the power to influence the mesocortical limbic circuitry, the very same circuit that helps us decide whether to take a risk.

When it comes to metacognition, not all people are created equal. Some of us are better at it than others. Steve Fleming, a neuroscientist at New York University, wondered if he might be able to quantify metacognition. So he and his colleagues recruited 32 volunteers to have their brains scanned as they made a simple perceptual choice: Which of two black and gray pictures was brighter? Of course, the two images were quite similar and the experimenters adjusted brightness levels to vary the amount of contrast between the two. But to get a handle on metacognition, or how self-aware participants were about their decisions, they then asked each to answer a simple question after choosing the brighter picture: On a scale from one to six, how sure are you of your answer?

Some people just seem to have a natural confidence about their choices—even when selecting between two very similar images. And when Fleming compared certainty to how well each partici-pant did in the perceptual task, he found that individuals who were pretty savvy about assessing their performance had slightly different brains from those who were not so savvy. Those with high self-awareness had a greater volume of gray matter, the dark matter of the brain that contains neurons and their connections, in part of the prefrontal cortex—our old friend, the brakes. In addition, they showed a stronger tract connection linking the prefrontal cortex to other parts of the brain. It would seem that being self-aware of your strengths and weaknesses has the power to influence key components of the risk-and-reward processing circuitry—and to help you make better decisions over time. But Fleming is quick to point out that these differences present a chicken-and-egg kind of scenario. It's possible that some folks just have a predisposition to strong metacognition. But it's equally as likely that these changes develop as folks gain more experience and get better at thinking about their thinking.

Of course, if asked, Baskin would argue that it's all about training and experience—that confidence comes from doing the work, working through different worst-case scenarios, and, yes, carefully reviewing your mistakes.

As Baskin explained, young neurosurgeons are trained to deal with the worst-case scenarios. They are constantly bombarded with "what-ifs" so they can make split-second decisions in the operating room. Yet, in watching Baskin work and in thinking about my own experiences with risk, I'd argue that good decision-making isn't just about that kind of training. Rather, the truth resides somewhere in the middle. Some of us, no matter how much training we have, are never going to have the kind of self-awareness and discipline that a man like Baskin has. I have to think that both nature and nurture play their part in helping us develop solid metacognition— the kind that's reliable enough to inform good decision-making when we are faced with uncertainty.

A SERIES OF ADJUSTMENTS

By the fifth hour of surgery, I'm slightly ashamed to say that I'm done. As Baskin and his team, slowly, surely, excise the tumor, bit by bit, I have to leave. I am called away to more mundane matters like school pickup and dinner fixings. And a much needed bathroom break. I'll be honest, I'm dead tired just from watching. But Baskin's team is pushing on, trying to cut faster than the tumor grows.

As I collect my belongings, I ask Baskin to follow up with me the next morning. Despite all the setbacks—and things were looking a little sticky upon my departure—I'm rooting for the patient. I'm hoping for the best of all outcomes. I want to see all that hard work and persistence pay off.

The next day, I hear from Baskin. He tells me that the surgical team continued to encounter significant bleeding throughout the rest of the surgery.

"We were stuck with a very difficult situation with continuous bleeding that could not be completely stopped. While one would ordinarily stage a procedure like this, stopping after a certain amount of blood loss, this was impossible here for two reasons," he explains. "First, while we could slow the bleeding to an ooze, we could not completely stop it. If we stopped and closed, she would have died from a clot in the brain. Second, unless we took most of the tumor out, there would be massive and likely fatal brain swelling."

I can see why neither option sounded particularly good. So the surgical team pressed on—for another 12 hours, to be exact. What was expected to be a 7- to 8-hour surgery turned into a 17-hour marathon, with 21 units of blood transfused into the patient over all that time. Yet, when all was said and done, Baskin was able to completely remove the tumor. "The patient is already awake and alert, following commands, with vision improved," he tells me. "With all the hurdles, it is a wonderful outcome." Ten days later, she walked out of the hospital with her vision completely restored.

While he is obviously pleased with the outcome, it's clear that Baskin sees this case as just another day in the life of a neurosurgeon. Risk-taking happens each and every day, he's quick to tell me, and in tough cases like this one, almost continuously. "There was lots of drama and many strategic decisions back and forth— with anesthesia, the nurses, and two doctors struggling not to lose the patient on the table. A lot of teamwork, snap life-and-death decisions, and stress."

Yet through it all, Baskin was able to successfully recover from any setbacks—and see the surgery through to the best possible outcome. When I consider the training, the preparation, the persistence, the control, and the self-awareness involved in dealing with errors, I find myself quite in awe. When I say so aloud, Baskin simply shrugs.

"When you try to accomplish anything in life, you have to have a healthy respect for how hard it might be. But, at the same time, you have to have enough energy, confidence, and motivation to propel yourself forward and make you certain you can do it," he sagely informs me. "At the end of the day, high-risk surgery is simply a series of adjustments. But, you know, most of life is."

He makes it sound so easy. And I must consider that maybe it really is that simple, whether you're talking brain surgery or baking.

A calculation of risk, followed by an informed series of adjustments in response to any setbacks. Successful recovery in the face of adversity, whether it be due to your own missteps or not, can be helped along by careful preparation, focusing on small wins, controlling what you can, being aware of your own strengths and weaknesses, and then letting go of past mistakes. Put those things together, and you're in a place where your mesocortical limbic circuitry is well synchronized with the world around you. Where you have the ability (and the right neurobiological prompts) to take a step back and put "catastrophic events" in the proper context for review. And that provides the kind of context that can help you learn, grow, and, yes, adjust accordingly, so you are better able to deal with risks the next time around. And that's something I'll remember the next time I feel outdone and overwhelmed by any task—even those silly ones involving Nutella.

PART IV

RISK, NOW AND FUTURE

Chapter Twelve

··

BUILDING THE BETTER RISK-TAKER

ONCE UPON A TIME, I WAS A RISK-TAKER. And, as I said, I'd like to be one again. A better risk-taker. A smarter risk-taker. The kind of risk-taker who can successfully leverage the risks I face to fully embrace life, liberty, and my own pursuit of happiness. I looked to both scientists and real-world risk-takers for some sensible, applicable lessons on how to do this very thing. And I hoped that those lessons, founded at the intersection of the laboratory and the real world, would help me better understand how I perceive and pursue risk when it really matters.

Given these lessons, have I learned how to build the better risk-taker? When I ask UT Austin's Tom Schonberg, the postdoctoral fellow who encourages scientists to bridge the gap between neuroeconomic and real-world risk-taking, what makes for an optimal risk-taker, he laughs at me. He's surprised that anyone would ask a neuroscientist for actual decision-making advice. But when I push, he does comes up with an answer—albeit a bit of a smug one.

"An optimal risk-taker is the guy who survives the 'hindsight is always 20-20' test," he tells me. "Unfortunately, you don't know if you made the right choice when you're taking the risk. The only real way to know is in hindsight. After you know how everything turned out."

Although the comment has a touch of smart-assery to it, he makes a valid point. The majority of the time, we don't know whether the risks we take will pan out or not. We won't and can't know. We can't even be sure if it was a "smart" risk. And that's an important lesson. There will always be risk in any decision. There will always be factors that are unknown and outside our control. The best we can do is risk enough over time, and gain the requisite knowledge, so we understand just what those factors are—and whether we are personally willing to deal with the potential consequences.

That said, I have learned quite a bit about building a better risk-taker as I've talked to scientists and successful risk-takers. To steal a line from G.I. Joe, "Knowing is half the battle." And the knowledge I've gleaned from the science and the real world has quite a bit to say about how we can take charge of risk, instead of letting risk take charge of us. We don't always have to be at risk's mercy. We can make it work for us. But doing so requires knowledge, focus, and awareness.

LESSON 1: RESET YOUR DEFINITION OF RISK

First and foremost, we need to start talking about risk in the right way.

Risk isn't gambling, extreme sports, junk bonds, or unprotected sex—though, certainly, those activities have elements of risk to them. Rather, risk is simply a decision or behavior that has a significant probability of resulting in a negative outcome. That's it. And it's time we accept that risk is part and parcel of every single decision we make, every single day—big or small, life-altering or seemingly inconsequential. There's risk involved in what you decide to eat for breakfast and in accepting a marriage proposal. There's risk involved in not paying your library fines and in speaking up at a big work meeting. There's risk involved in falling in love and in ending a relationship. Don't even get me started on the risks involved with raising children. There's risk in going out into the world. And there's risk in staying home. Risk is everywhere. It's time to acknowledge that very few decisions in life come with any sort of guaranteed outcome. Pretending risk is something than can be left to other people— you know, *real* risk-takers like professional poker players, firefighters, teenagers, BASE jumpers, community advocates, entrepreneurs, Special Forces operators, or brain surgeons—does none of us any favors. It makes risk seem like something out of the ordinary—and a lot scarier than it has to be. Over time, those kinds of exaggerated notions can get in the way of us making smart decisions.

Let me let you in on a little secret. Given that risk is part of everyday decision-making, we—you, your spouse, your mom, your boss, even that guy who started biting his nails just reading through Chapter Seven—are risk-takers. Every single one of us. I said that once upon a time, I was a risk-taker. But, as it turns out, I never stopped being one. I couldn't have stopped even if I wanted to. Despite the fact I was no longer skydiving or wandering the globe, I was still making decisions. Even suburbia, as boring as it may be, requires you to partake in some basic risk management to survive (or, at least, to avoid the wrath of the homeowner's association). And so, despite myself, I remain a risk-taker—albeit a different sort of risk-taker than I was in my 20s. You are also a risk-taker. And it's time we all admit as much—and accept risk for what it is, not what it has been inflated into.

Rutgers neuroscientist Mauricio Delgado, who studies how emotions and stress affect risk-taking, will be the first to tell you that risk-taking is part of normal decision-making. And, for him, successful risk-taking is simply about being willing to explore alternatives.

"When you do that, you learn from your experiences. You learn to adapt your behavior so you know how to weigh the risks against the consequences," he says. "And, over time, by taking some risks—in the context of a long-term goal—you learn how to make better decisions."

I think most of us would appreciate learning how to make better decisions. But there's more to this risk reset than just knocking our definition of risk back into size—or understanding how important it is to even the most minimal of decisions. We also need to stop talking about risk in extremes.

You know what I mean: Risk is bad; it can lead to danger and death. Risk is good; it can lead to glory and happiness. We need to find a bit of a happy medium here. Because, more and more, scientists are learning that risk is neither good nor bad. Rather, they're finding that risk-taking is *necessary.* Remember that old adage "Good experience comes from bad judgment?" It's more than just a catchy expression. Risk-taking is an integral part of the brain's learning system. It is there to push on boundaries and help us learn and adapt. Sticking with the status quo does us no favors. Risk offers us potential—the kind of potential that can help us grow, explore, and respond to the world around us. And that provides a platform to help us make the right changes to successfully go after the things we most want (and need) in life.

LESSON 2: KNOW WHAT YOU CAN'T CHANGE

Once you accept that everyone is a risk-taker, the next step is to recognize what kind of risk-taker you are. Both science (and life) make it clear that each of us, with our own unique blend of biology and bravado, will approach risky situations differently. As J. Koji Lum, the genetic anthropologist from Binghamton University, tells me, our different genetic makeups mean that our mesocortical limbic circuits will work just a little bit differently. And, consequently, our risk-taking algorithms, the internal calculations that determine how we'll handle danger and uncertainty when we encounter it, will operate at slightly different frequencies. Over time, Lum argues, those small differences result in very different lives lived.

That's why you'll see people who always seem to grab on to risks with both hands—and those who try to avoid risks at all costs. And, of course, every variation of risk-taking behavior in between. Individual differences play a key role in how we perceive and respond to risk as we make decisions. And if you want to become a better risk-taker, you have to figure out what your default algorithms are. You have to know if you are one of those people who needs to exert more effort to pump the brakes when faced with new risks—or the person who needs a push to start thinking about stepping on the gas pedal at all.

I can't change my genetic makeup. That was a gift from my parents—and one that I'll carry with me for the rest of my life. Their combined genes helped to shape my mesocortical limbic circuitry, as well as my innate risk-taking algorithms. Similarly, I can't change my sex or my age. To better vet risk, I need to give a nod to serenity and accept my natural-born risk-taker—and exercise a little self-awareness. As simple as that sounds, self-awareness can help you better manage risk too.

For example, in a recent study of executive leaders done by Green Peak Partners in conjunction with Cornell's School of Industrial and Labor Relations, researchers found that scoring high on self-awareness measures was the best predictor at overall business success. Business leaders who understood their own strengths and weaknesses were better able to manage risk at work. And certainly, I've seen the same in the successful risk-takers I've come to know and love. Self-awareness is not always easy. But knowing what you can't change—who you are and how you innately respond to risk—leads to better, smarter choices when you consider a risky decision. It can help you learn when to let go and when to press on. And it can help put risk in proper context, so you can leverage it to achieve your long-term goals.

Are you the kind of person who tends to act impulsively? Or do you always think things through—maybe a little too far through? Are you a sensation-seeker, always on the lookout for thrills and adventure? Or do you prefer the comforts of home? Are you in thrall to novelty? Or are you someone who delights in the familiar? Look at the way you tend to make decisions, the patterns that make up your life, to see what they tell you about the kind of risk-taker you are. No matter how you answered these questions, you have it within you to be a successful risk-taker. We all do. But you have to know your baseline—your instinctive response to risk—so you can better understand when you may be pressing too hard on the gas or the brakes. And that kind of self-knowledge will help ensure that you are vetting risk in a way that will ultimately bring you closer to your goals—of both the short- and long-term variety.

LESSON 3: KNOW WHAT YOU CAN CHANGE

Understanding your inner risk-taker is only the first step. After all, genetic predisposition or no, biology does not exist in a vacuum.

No discussion of risk-taking would be complete without considering the environmental factors that we encounter—and that we can alter as needed. As we've seen, things like familiarity, social groups, emotion, stress, and recovery have the power to influence risk-taking algorithms. We cannot discount their reach—and how they can transform the way we calculate risks in our day-to-day lives. But once again, those transformations can be better managed with a little awareness.

Russ Poldrack, a researcher at UT Austin who studies risk and decision-making, tells me that a good risk-taker is never brash or reckless. "We often talk about impulsivity and risk-taking in the same breath. But they are clearly different," he says. "The successful risk-taker is thoughtful and prepared. Functional risk-taking is about reasoned risks and an adjusted temporal horizon. It's likely that the successful risk-taker is taking risks that help him move toward a long-term goal, whereas the dysfunctional risk-taker is only looking at immediate outcomes."

Successful risk-takers are planners by nature. They don't fly by the seat of their pants—they consider all the factors. They visualize success. They focus on the big picture. They understand that any big move is only a series of smaller, more digestible steps. They take their time, they prepare, and they take only the risks that help them reach their larger, long-term goals. And, in the end, that's what helps to ensure that they succeed more often than they fail.

Each of us has those same powers at our disposal. We can look to the environmental factors we can control—and take a moment to consider how they may be influencing how we decide. Once we do, we can use that awareness to inform better decisions.

Preparation*.* Because of their consistent and often intense training, successful risk-takers are prepared for any contingency. And that's because they have the requisite education to recognize exactly what the contingencies are. They are aware of the best way to respond to different risky situations. They understand how even the smallest change in the environment can change the entire risk-taking equation. They spend an inordinate amount of time training and practicing so what they do feels like second nature. All that learning—and deliberate practice—syncs up their fast- and slow-thinking systems, which leads to smarter decision-making.

Time and time again, researchers have found that risk-taking is inordinately influenced by how familiar we are with the activity at hand. If your peers are engaging in a particular behavior—whether it be smoking pot, drag racing, or running off to an ashram in India—you won't perceive it as overwhelmingly risky. So what's the first thing to do when faced with a risky decision? Get familiar. Take some time, do your homework, and get to know an activity so you can understand the true scope of the risks involved.

Then, if it is something you decide to pursue, practice—and practice deliberately. Learn how to adapt your mind and body to the situation at hand. Practice enough so that you can build the kind of intuition you can count on—instead of the flimsier feelings you can't. Practice so that you can develop decision-making heuristics and habits that will help you learn, grow, and, ultimately, choose wisely.

Connection*.* As social beings, we cannot discount the power of social influence in how, where, and why we take risks. Even familiarity has a social component—if our friends are happily engaging in certain behaviors, we aren't as likely to perceive them as risky even when they are. Our social connections—family, friends, co-workers, and even that hot guy at the library that you're desperate to talk to—sway us when we make decisions. They can amplify the perception of a reward, leading us to pump the gas. Or they can threaten us with social isolation, which can lead to more brake-like behaviors. And as Ruth Murray-Webster, the corporate risk consultant, explains, just being aware of how social groups can affect your decision-making is one of the most important things you can do to make sure their influence isn't working to your detriment.

When faced with a risk, take a step back and, as objectively as possible, consider how your social connections may be driving your focus. Are they helping you consider all the elements of a risky decision? Or are they stuck on certain variables that may lead you astray? Are they allowing transparency and challenges to the status quo? Or are they closed off to any criticism? Murray-Webster argues that just taking a moment to examine how your social groups may be driving your decisions can help counteract any negative influences.

Emotion and stress. Life can be overwhelming—as can many of the important decisions we need to make concerning love, work, and life in general. It's clear that both stress and emotion have the ability to alter the way we consider risks. If you aren't aroused enough, you probably won't have the motivation to do much of anything. But if you're too aroused, you'll find yourself with a skewed, probably detrimental risk calculation—one that places too much emphasis on affect-rich outcomes. Luckily, it's equally as clear that each one of us holds the power to self-regulate our more overwhelming feelings.

For example, when Wall Street trader turned professional poker player Andrew Frankenberger played heads-up against Phil Ivey, largely considered the best poker player in the world, he didn't give into fear or stress. Despite his passion for competition (and winning), he put on his slow-thinking cap and considered the outcome if the worst were to happen.

"Ivey is such an intimidating opponent. He's so good. And for me, when I played him, I knew there was no downside. No one expected me to win. There's more pressure to beat Joe Schmo than there is to beat Phil Ivey," he explains. "If I lost, everyone would have just said, 'Hey, nice try. You lost to the best.' And I would have just been excited that I had the opportunity to play with him."

That kind of self-regulation is extremely valuable—and likely helped Frankenberger take Ivey down at that World Series of Poker final table. By considering the downsides, he was able to deemphasize the emotion of the event and play to his best ability. Luckily, there are myriad ways to de-emphasize your decisions—whether you are playing Phil Ivey or just encountering run-of-the-mill emotional or stressful situations. Scientists have shown that meditation, training, visualization, and simple breathing techniques can work. Even a simple "Relax" cue can do the trick. You can figure out which method works best for you. But by utilizing cognitive strategies to engage the slow-thinking system, you can balance out the faster one when you are overwhelmed by stress or emotion—and that will lead to better decisions all around.

Recovery. Failure, when it comes to future risk-taking, is a gift. Successful risk-takers are often motivated by failure—it's what tells them that they aren't done preparing yet. It's inspiration to work harder, to train better, and to learn more. They understand that mistakes have the potential to offer them as much, if not more, than success in the way of both data and experience. They don't take failure as a sign to stop and set their sights on something new. Instead, they manage to regulate their emotional response to it, place errors in the proper context, and learn what they can from those mistakes to better reach their ultimate goal.

Each of us has the power to do the same. Instead of making a mistake and throwing in the towel, we can review the circumstances around the failure. We can ask ourselves what we might have missed—or what factors we should have given more credence to. And instead of wallowing in our ineptitude, we can put those errors in the context of our larger goals. And then, if we let them, our mistakes can show us how to do better next time.

David Baskin, the neurosurgeon, told me that surgery, much like life, is merely a series of adjustments. He sees it as one of the reasons why he is so successful in his field: He adjusts. We, too, can adjust. And part of that adjustment is taking our failures in stride and finding ways to leverage them in future risky decisions.

When I ask Steph Davis, the BASE jumper, about how she feels about not finishing a project, or failing to complete a big climbing goal, she tells me succinctly, "I don't see it as failure. I'm just not done yet."

It's likely, as you face different risks as you approach a big goal, you just aren't done yet either. The trick is realizing it.

LESSON 4: TAKE THE LEAP

When I first set out to research and write this book, I had hoped to give it some kind of cinematic ending. Maybe I'd try BASE jumping or book some kind of eco-adventure in Southeast Asia. I'd be so inspired by all that I'd learned about risk-taking that I'd get over my middle-aged reservations about safety and start mixing it up again. And, of course, as I embarked on these new adventures, I'd have the full support of my new family. Maybe I'd even drag them along for the ride.

That's right: new family. Because I, the divorced (and gun-shy) single mom, found myself more than considering my boyfriend's proposal, despite the fact we'd known each other such a short time. Just a few weeks after my boyfriend asked if I would have him, I happily—and unreservedly—accepted his proposal. From the outside, I'm sure it looked like we broke one of the cardinal risk-taking rules and acted rather impulsively. Many thought we should wait, another year, maybe longer, to make sure we were doing the right thing. They argued that we hadn't put enough of our focus on the long-term. That we were pumping the gas without properly manning the brakes. But, from the inside, that was far from the case. We had both learned some powerful and painful lessons during our first marriages. And those were things we were willing to apply in our own relationship. From the get-go, we understood what we absolutely did not want in a partner. But we had also figured out what we each desperately needed in one. Before saying yes, I drilled him on how he'd handle every hypothetical marriage-straining situation I could imagine—from acting on requests outlined in a living will to what kinds of clothing can safely go in the dryer. While he may need a little more instruction on the laundry front, we found that we saw eye-to-eye on just about everything else. By engaging in some self-awareness (and exercising both my fast- and my slow-thinking systems in the process), I quickly realized that this was a man who was willing to meet me halfway as a true partner. And I'd be risking more, a hell of a lot more, if I let him go. So I did what you are supposed to do after you've looked carefully at your cards, evaluated your fellow players, and realized that, to the best of your knowledge, you have the best hand at the table. I went all in.

Three months later, a rather hippie-esque man in a Hawaiian shirt married us on a Florida beach at sunset. It was a rather simple affair. There were no guests, save our two children and a random young family enjoying the last vestiges of sunshine near the water. We took only a handful of photos—mostly as a new family rather than as a couple. I trashed my dress in the surf and immediately threw it down the garbage chute once we finished. We followed our union by a late dinner at a chain steakhouse, because it had the shortest wait and we forgot to make reservations anywhere else. The flowers came from the supermarket and I completely blanked on cake or champagne. Yet, in our vows, we both commemorated the leap we were taking— and the risks involved. I promised to not see our mistakes as failures but as opportunities to learn. He vowed to always try new things with me, as long as they are legal in the applicable jurisdiction. And we both promised to listen, love, and do the work. All told, I can't think of a better way to end a midlife crisis in reverse.

Except, perhaps, to add in a little BASE jumping. I really sort of missed the opportunity to give you a real action-hero kind of ending by not doing that. My apologies. But here's the thing: It would not have been genuine. It would not have really represented what I learned about smart risk-taking. Because for the vast majority of us, risk management is not about BASE jumping or neurosurgery or $10,000 buy-in poker tournaments. A choice few of us, maybe. But for the rest of us, intelligent risk calculation is simply about letting yourself get out of your comfort zone every once in a while so you can explore new options. Options that may have the potential to help you learn, grow, and realize your long-term goals. My big dreams aren't about extreme sports. But they do involve a few other risky ventures—saying yes to a new family, writing this book, traveling more, and finding novel (albeit sometimes fairly mundane) ways to extract my ass from the couch.

Optimal risk-taking doesn't have to be about thrill-seeking or even about exotic adventure. As Mauricio Delgado, the Rutgers risk researcher, tells me, even small risks, something as simple as choosing a new restaurant, have value. Risk-taking is not about death-defying feats or million-dollar investments. It's about exploring, adapting, focusing, and making predictions about future experiences. And, therefore, risk-taking is a critical part of learning and memory and being alive.

I've learned that healthy, clever risk-taking doesn't have to be complicated—it can be as simple as taking a new route to work, trying the new sushi place that opened up downtown, taking up a new hobby, traveling (even in your own backyard), or meeting new people. What risk-taking is really about is challenging yourself a bit so you can accrue wisdom and help your brain become a better, more efficient prediction machine. It's about gathering enough knowledge and experience so you understand the potential ins and outs of any situation you encounter. It's about keeping your brain sharp—and being prepared to deal with whatever life throws at you. It's about recognizing the importance of context, running collected data through both your fast and slow systems, and coming up with the best decision with the information at hand.

When I look inside myself, and exercise that critical self-awareness, I realize that risk-taking, for me, isn't about something like jumping out of an airplane anymore. That's not what I love; it's not the kind of thing that fires me up and motivates me to get out of bed in the morning. But what does move me is the idea of expanding my business and my family. Traveling to new places and teaching my kids to appreciate experiences over possessions. Making mistakes—but putting them in proper context so that I can leverage those blunders in such a way to help me reach my goals. And, yes, taking a page from P!nk, working harder to turn off that *Law and Order* marathon so I can ensure my life is more like what I envisioned it would be like when I was 16. And to do that, I'll happily take the advice of the successful risk-takers I met—and put a more concerted effort into making some smart risks of my own, come what may.

I don't know what might move you. But I'll hazard a guess that, if you think about it for a moment, you have more than an inkling. G.I. Joe was right. When it comes to risk, knowing *is* half the battle. And by knowing yourself and what you want most from life—as well as knowing how your environment can influence you as you try to reach those goals—you have the power to take charge of risk and follow it to more success.

With that in mind, maybe it's time for you to let go of your more outdated notions about risk-taking. Maybe it's time to look deep within yourself and better understand what kind of natural risk-taker you are. As you look around your environment and take stock of the factors that influence your decision-making, perhaps you should start adding a few more calculated risks to your life. Risks that will help you stay sharp, learn, grow, and reach your most cherished dreams, whatever they happen to be. And maybe, just maybe, it's time to start now.

ACKNOWLEDGMENTS

WHERE TO BEGIN? Although writing seems, at most times, to be a very solitary endeavor, so many people contributed to this book. I'm afraid I'll never properly thank them all.

I am forever indebted to the many researchers who contributed their time and expertise to this project—even allowing me to visit their labs and try some laboratory risk-taking for myself. Many thanks to Sarah Helfinstein, Tom Schonberg, and Russ Poldrack for their willingness to talk data and the implications for real-world risk-takers—as well as to give me a go at the BART. I'm still twitching a bit. Thanks to J. Koji Lum for giving me the ammunition to deny my mother's assertion that I am genetically destined for trouble. And Abby Baird, I could spend hours picking your brain and never get tired. Neuroscientists, truly, are not only wicked smart but also wicked fun.

I am also grateful to the dozens of other scientists who discussed their fascinating research over the course of this project, including Chris Chabris, Craig Ferris, C. Daniel Salzman, Michael Frank, Joshua Buckholtz, Jeff Cooper, Emrah Duezel, Marvin Zuckerman, Wolfram Schultz, Mauricio Delgado, Ann Graybiel, Thomas Kelly, Justin Garcia, Margareta Bohlin, Charles Limb, Scott Grafton,

Bernd Figner, Michael Posner, James Bursley, Erik Dane, Ruth Murray-Webster, Marius Usher, Barry Komisaruk, Gareth Jones, Ulrich Mayr, Thomas Hills, Ming Hsu, Jon-Kar Zubieta, Jordan Grafman, Paul Slovic, Jerome Kagan, Doreen Arcus, Rod Duclos, Bita Moghaddam, and Ronald Dahl. Your collective brilliance and kindness has offered me more than I can ever repay.

And, of course, my risk-takers were equally as amazing. Thanks to Michelle, Leah Davis, Steph Davis, Andy Frankenberger, Jonathan, Mark Walters, John Danner, Gayle King, and David Baskin. You are all so amazing—and have inspired me to start taking more smart risks myself. Thanks also to Stoya and Corrine for their time and thoughts.

Thanks to my agent, Joy Tutela, for always having my back. And also to Nicky Penttila, a brilliant editor and good friend, for her notes on the manuscript. To the supersecret Board, your comments (both related and unrelated) were also greatly appreciated. And thanks to Susan Tyler Hitchcock, Hilary Black, and the rest of the team at National Geographic Books for shaping this book into something worth reading.

In the depths of book-writing purgatory, my friends and family offered me their insights, love, and encouragement. They also offered wine, chocolate, and funny cat photos. Thank you to Sarah Rose, Dave Dillon, Helen King, Rebekah Sanderlin, Alison Buckholtz, Sylvia Hauser, Sue Baker, Jody Mace, Beth Bailie, Stacy Lu, the TEDMED and Chicago Ideas teams, Chester Cheetah, Megan Hughes, Susannah Cahalan, Victoria Loustalot, Alex George, Manisha Gupta, Gwen Moran, Jen Singer, Laura Laing, the Wests, the Schills, the Gilberts, and the Place-Gateaus for, well, everything.

- *Acknowledgments* -

And thanks to all my friends, real and virtual, on both Twitter and Facebook. Your support, insights, and answers to hypothetical risk-taking questions made all the difference.

Roan Low, what can I say? You are my rock.

But, most of all, thank you to my family. For putting up with me, mainly—but also for inspiring me to live well, no matter the risk involved. Laurel, thank you for accepting my inner risk-taker, even if she isn't particularly ladylike. Chet, your unique mix of heart and fearlessness mean that we'll always find new adventures together. Ella, you are the daughter I always dreamed of having. I'm so glad I get to be your bonus Mom.

And Dion, my love—for you, I go all in. And I always will.

INDEX

ABOUT THE AUTHOR

Kayt Sukel earned a B.S. in cognitive psychology from Carnegie Mellon University and an M.S. in engineering psychology from the Georgia Institute of Technology. A passionate traveler and science writer, she is the author of the critically acclaimed book *This Is Your Brain on Sex: The Science Behind the Search for Love* (Free Press, 2013). In addition, her essays and articles have appeared in the *The Atlantic,* the *New Scientist, USA Today,* the *Washington Post, Islands, Parenting,* the *Bark, Pacific Standard, Proto, American Baby,* and *Scientific American Mind.* Sukel is a frequent contributor to the Dana Foundation's many publications, and her science writing frequently appears online. Much of it—including stories about out-of-body experiences, hands-free orgasms, new stem cell technologies, and exotic travel with young children—can be found on her own website, kaytsukel.com. She lives in Houston, Texas (and is as surprised about it as you are), and frequently overshares on Twitter as @kaytsukel.